When Money
Was in
Fashion

When Money Was in Fashion

HENRY GOLDMAN,

GOLDMAN SACHS, AND THE

FOUNDING OF WALL STREET

JUNE BRETON FISHER

palgrave
macmillan

Photograph of the original Goldman Sachs building is reproduced courtesy of Goldman Sachs

Photograph of the Goldman and Sachs family gathering in Elberon, New Jersey is provided courtesy of Goldman Sachs

Photographs of Goldman family members are provided courtesy of the author

WHEN MONEY WAS IN FASHION
Copyright © June Breton Fisher, 2010.

First published in 2010 by
PALGRAVE MACMILLAN™
175 Fifth Avenue, New York, N.Y. 10010 and
Houndmills, Basingstoke, Hampshire, England RG21 6XS.
Companies and representatives throughout the world.

PALGRAVE MACMILLAN is the global academic imprint of the Palgrave Macmillan division of St. Martin's Press, LLC and of Palgrave Macmillan Ltd. Macmillan® is a registered trademark in the United States, United Kingdom and other countries. Palgrave is a registered trademark in the European Union and other countries.

ISBN-13: 978-0-230-61750-6

Library of Congress Cataloging-in-Publication Data is available from the Library of Congress.

A catalogue record of the book is available from the British Library.

Design by Letra Libre

First edition: May 2010
10 9 8 7 6 5 4 3 2 1
Printed in the United States of America.

Contents

꒰ V ꒱

Acknowledgments

A number of people have contributed to the creation of this book, and I owe each and every one a vote of thanks. I am especially grateful to my friend Dan Alef, without whose encouragement and interest I would never have started—or finished—the book; Victoria Skurnick, my wonderful agent, who gave me faith in myself and wrote such a great pitch on my behalf; my publisher and editor, Airié Stuart, whose advice transformed an assortment of rambling verbal snapshots into a meaningful portrait of an extraordinary man unknown by the public; the ever-patient Marie Ostby and Leah Carroll, for fielding unending questions about the minutiae of the publishing world; David Rotstein, who designed the wonderful jacket; and Kathleen Laman, along with Ardis Parshall, for their assistance in typing the manuscript.

Peter Thompson and Ed Canaday, of Goldman Sachs, gave me invaluable access to the archives at Goldman Sachs.

Mayor Kurt Mauer, of Trappstadt, Germany, and his friends Elizabeth Bohrer and Michael B shared their extensive knowledge of the Goldman and Sachs family backgrounds, genealogy, and early history.

Arthur and Mary Sachs filled in the cracks.

The following people were also invaluable in my research: Mark Henderson and Kate Ralston of the Getty Research Institute; Charis Shafer and her staff at the Oral Research Department at Columbia University; Charles Griefenstein of the American Philosophical Society; Anna Lee Pauls and Charles Greene of Princeton University; Barbara Wolff of the Hebrew University in Jerusalem, Israel; Mary Hotaling of the Adirondack Historical Society, who made available material on Albert Einstein, Joseph Duveen, Yehudi Menuhin, Max Born, and members of the Sachs family who are long since gone.

Barbara Cohen and her daughter, Marcia, shared family photographs from their private collection.

Wolfgang Grahl provided excellent translations of correspondence from Germany.

The staff of the Montecito, California, Public Library were unfailingly helpful in tracking down the innumerable books that I used in my research.

And, of course, my daughter, journalist Tracy Breton, for her research assistance.

And last but not least, I need to thank my mother, who kept the family photographs in pristine order and remembered the stories.

Preface

Ever since my fourth-grade teacher spun tales of the pharaohs and the treasures buried with them inside the pyramids, I have harbored a wild desire to dig and discover secrets of my own. They say archeology is in your blood—my great-aunt Hetty was a famed Mesopotamiast who participated in significant excavations in Greece and Turkey in the 1920s and 30s and was the first woman fellow in the humanities department of the Institute for Advanced Study. But I never saw Egypt or the land of the *Iliad* until I was well into middle age, and by then my intellectual curiosity had become more focused on a subject closer to my real-time life, my grandfather Henry Goldman, the iconic, innovative co-leader of the great firm Goldman Sachs, and America's first investment banker.

The world was familiar by then with his many and varied exploits, although he had made every effort to maintain anonymity while achieving his goals. I, a virtual fly on the wall, young and precocious, had not only known him personally, but had also been witness to his relationships with a fascinating mix of people, many of whom were changing the world in one way or another. I now wanted to peel back the layers of secrecy swaddling his persona and show him to the world.

And so began a three-year journey that has taken me to Philadelphia, New York, Berlin, Dresden, St. Moritz, Paris, Baden-Baden, and Trappstadt, the little Bavarian village where it all began.

Henry Goldman

Although a few of the incidents contained in my story are simply based on educated hearsay, notably the link-up of Marcus Goldman and Joseph Sachs in Philadelphia, all the events and characters are real and, for the most part, speak for themselves.

CHAPTER ONE

Against All Odds

"Men can learn from the past, and I've been shocked how little some of the younger executives in the present firm know about its origins. They don't even know that my grandfather whose picture is on the wall there founded the firm."

—Walter Sachs, senior partner of Goldman Sachs, 1928[1]

My grandfather, Henry Goldman, was the son of a poor German immigrant named Marcus Goldmann who was born in 1821 in Trappstadt, one of a number of small villages that dot the rolling green wheat fields and dense forests of the Bavarian countryside. Marcus was the eldest child of Wolf Goldmann, a farmer and cattle dealer, who was married to a young woman by the name of Bella Katz Oberbrunner from the neighboring town of Zeil am Main. She had already had five children by her first husband, Samuel, when he died at the age of thirty-seven.

Trappstadt, the Bavarian village where Marcus was born, 1840s

The family name had not always been Goldmann. According to the decree of the Catholic diocese of nearby Würzburg, which had ruled the region since the eleventh century, Jews did not have surnames and were known only by their given names and those of their fathers, and thus Wolf's father originally bore the name of Jonathan Marx, or more correctly, "Jonathan son of Marx." But in 1811, at the age of fifty-eight, when the Church revised its mandates and required the Jewish population to assume family names, Jonathan chose Goldmann, identifying it with the wealth and respected reputation of the elder citizen who officiated at his son Wolf's wedding.

Wolf was their first child, a restless, ambitious young man with a thirst for education who found the city walls of his hometown far too confining. The family home was located just around the corner from the local schoolhouse, and when he finished helping his father in the barnyard and the garden, Wolf would sneak into the back of the classroom and absorb as much as he could of the day's lessons in bookkeeping, reading, and history.

Although surrounded by vineyards and already well regarded as a center for breweries, Zeil offered virtually no opportunities for Jews to earn an independent living. Restrictive municipal laws, in fact, forbade Jews from voting, marrying, or having children, and so Wolf plotted from an early age to leave his family homestead and move closer to Bamberg, a larger, more progressive city sixteen miles away. However, in 1813 the Catholic diocese had imposed quotas on the number of Jews allowed to settle in each of the minuscule villages of the region, and to ensure compliance charged "protection money" from those who were granted residence permits. These measures virtually eliminated the possibility of a Jew's relocating to another township unless he replaced a dead man on the census rolls. Wolf started to haunt the record hall in Würzburg, which listed the names of Jews who had recently been interred and the villages in which they had resided. After many months of fruitless checking, he spotted the name of Samuel Oberbrunner, a young cattle dealer from the market town of Trappstadt, who had passed away shortly after the first of the year. He was survived by a wife, Ella, and five children ranging from four to eleven years of age. Investigating further, Wolf found that the young widow had not been left enough money to hire someone who could help tend the livestock that provided the family's livelihood. Recognizing that he and Ella had compatible needs, Wolf presented himself at the kitchen door of her house, which was simply identified as Number 16, and suggested that he work for her as a hired hand in exchange for his room and board.

The couple was married six months later in Sternberg, where Ella had grown up, as there was no synagogue in Trappstadt. Who knows whether it was a marriage of love or convenience or a combination of the two? They led a contented family life for forty years and had five more children, four of whom survived. Mark, the eldest, was born in 1822, Samuel (who died as an infant) two years later, and then another boy, Simon, and two girls, Bella and Regina. The family moved to a larger home near the town cemetery and the synagogue, where there was a growing colony of fifty-three Jews in residence, and the family cattle business thrived.

His stepsisters all made a fuss over Mark—after all, there were five of them, and for years he was the only boy! But he remained sweet natured and obedient, and was never known to give his parents any trouble. He loved school and was a good student, particularly adept at mathematics. His brother Simon, four years his junior, was his total antithesis: mischievous, volatile, doing his daily chores only after persistent nagging. Nevertheless, the boys were close to each other and looked forward to the monthly market days in the village when they helped their father sell his cattle. People from all the surrounding villages streamed into the main square for the occasion, and the town had the feeling of a big, jolly party.

Every spring their father took them to the larger district market in Bamberg, nine miles away. They rose while it was still dark to herd the cattle up and down rutted dirt paths that meandered through the pastoral terrain. Simon was sometimes inclined to whine and complain, but Papa would shush him with fanciful tales about the glamorous lives of the Baron and Baroness von Henneberg, who governed the area, and Mark would sing folk tunes he had learned from Hungarian gypsies passing through town. Any thoughts of being tired or having sore feet vanished once they reached the outskirts of the city.

Bamberg rose like a fairyland between the river Regnitz and a canal that was crossed by several wooden bridges. A lock and a weir, situated below the tall frescoed town hall, took pride of place in the middle of town. Half-timbered and baroque houses in ice cream shades of peach and sandstone and pistachio green, all with red tile roofs, lined the winding narrow cobblestone streets—so narrow that the boys sometimes spotted the fire brigade answering alarms on bicycles rather than horse-drawn wagons. Beautiful stone and plaster representations of saints and angels decorated the outside walls of many houses they passed. And rising above everything was the cathedral, with its spires and impressive stained-glass windows. Once in a while the boys would peek inside and gawk at the likeness of the city's founder astride his horse, which had been carved into the wall of the nave many centuries earlier.

The market was held at the Maximiliansplatz, the largest square in the city. Every imaginable fruit and vegetable was sold there—fat white asparagus and luscious strawberries, and mushrooms, pota- toes, cauliflower, and cabbages harvested in fall. Around the corner, overlooked by the *Gabelmann,* or Neptune Fountain, there was a large flower market where ladies from the surrounding manor houses sent their servants to fill baskets with roses, lilies, and mar- guerites. Downstream from the town hall and the Benedictine monastery, in "Little Venice," colorful half-timbered fishermen's houses with neat little gardens and tiny balconies were lined up like a stage set facing the river. The cattle market and the municipal slaughterhouse were located nearby.

While Wolf negotiated the best prices for his cattle—and he was known to be a master at bartering—the two boys skipped stones on the river and watched the local toughs competing in rowing races and jousting as they balanced in canoes. At the closing bell, Papa would drop in to one of the many beer kellers on the street—there were sixty-five of them within the city, some over a hundred years old—for a pint and a pipe and to gossip with other farmers who had come to town for market day. The conversation was always spirited and spiked with acrimony about the peasants' lack of representation in the government, the economic havoc wreaked by endless wars among Germany's many feudal states, the punishing taxes from which only the rich seemed to benefit. And, not least, the "blood money" extracted by the government to obtain papers allowing those from the less privileged classes to emigrate in search of a better life.

The Goldmann children were devoted to one another, the older girls taking care of the little ones and assisting with the household chores while the boys tended the animals and helped their father in the fields. Once they reached the age of six, both boys and girls attended a "mixed" school for Christian and Jewish children and were taught history, geography, simple arithmetic, and a smattering of English. Wolf was especially proud of Mark, who, at the age of sixteen, had been encouraged by the schoolmaster to make periodic trips to the Würzburg synagogue, where the rabbi offered more advanced classes to outstanding students. It was there that Mark made the acquaintance of Joseph Sachs, the nineteen-year-old son of a poor saddle maker. Joseph had determined at an early age that he wanted to make a career of teaching school. The two young men became fast friends, never dreaming that their futures would be entwined for more than a century in a land they had yet to see.

At the time, Joseph was boarding in the home of a rich Würzburg goldsmith by the name of Baer, where he had been engaged to tutor the young lady of the house, Sophia. Ignoring her parents' staunch disapproval, she developed a crush on her teacher, and a storybook romance developed. They secretly pooled Joseph's meager savings with the jewelry Sophia had received from her parents since her birth and eloped one night to the port of Hamburg. There they stayed at the home of one of her cousins and were married several weeks later. Then, with little more than his tutoring credentials in his battered suitcase, Joseph set sail for Philadelphia, first circling South America with his plucky and adoring bride at his side. The journey lasted six weeks.

It had become increasingly apparent that there was no future for young Jewish men in Germany. Their station in society was lower than that of the Negro in pre–Civil War America. Rumblings of uprisings against the monarchy were becoming louder and increasingly passionate, jobs were almost nonexistent, and a year-long drought had resulted in poor harvests and a devastating famine. In addition, the likelihood of all able-bodied men being conscripted for military service in support of governments reluctant to recognize their basic rights seemed probable. Wolf reluctantly concluded it was time for his eldest son, who had just turned twenty-seven, to seek a new start in the United States.

The Bamberg newspaper had run stories almost every day about the grand opportunities available to newcomers in America, the warm welcome they were receiving, the fairness and freedom of a democratic society. In fact, a recent article had told of an orphan boy named Levi Strauss from a nearby village who had left the Old World and peddled fabrics from a backpack when he got off the boat. Soon afterward, he made a fortune sewing work pants for gold prospectors heading out west. As Mark deliberated and demurred, concerned that his parents would find running the farm without his help too heavy a load, twenty-three-year-old Simon, entranced with

the vision of gold lying on the streets of California, impulsively volunteered to keep him company.

On the eve of Mark and Simon's departure in 1848, Ella baked
the family's favorite apple cake and Wolf gave both of his sons his
blessings and 150 gulden to tide them over until they were settled.
There were no regrets, no long-drawn-out farewells. In the morning, Mark and Simon registered for exit papers with the town clerk
at the village Rathaus and paid a hefty "Jewish tax" on top of the
$50 charge for train tickets to Bremerhaven and passage on the
steamship *Miles* to London. There they would board the *Margaret
Evans,* bound for Philadelphia, the City of Brotherly Love, which
was surrounded by verdant farmland and offered a myriad of employment opportunities to immigrants. It was said to have a sizable
German population and was hospitable to Christians, Muslims, and
Jews alike.

The *Miles* was packed to the gunwales with German émigrés
when the halyards were set free and she drew away from the dock.
An unexpectedly large increase in the German population over the
past few years had fostered a move to stimulate emigration with cash
rewards, which were freely disbursed among doctors, lawyers, musicians, teachers, and artists. All the proletariat, in fact, except those
of the Jewish faith. Unacceptable as they may have been, they alone
were required to buy their way out.

As the ship's white sails unfurled and she drew out of the harbor,
the passengers gathered on deck to have a last glimpse of their homeland and sang a sad song of farewell. "A proud ship goes lonely,"
went the refrain, "taking our German brothers away . . . to America.

Poor Germany, do you want to banish us to live the rest of our lives and die in America? We have nowhere else to go and our choice would be to stay. Don't forget us. We shall return someday."

It was an extremely rough night crossing the Channel, and the brothers spent most of the voyage clinging to the railing on the upper deck. London showed them few of her charms, and they spent the early hours of the morning searching the port through a pea soup fog for the *Margaret Evans*. When at last they signed on board, they were assigned quarters measuring six by six feet, which they were to share with two other émigrés, a British machinist and a brewmaster from Munich, who was planning to join the gold rush and make his fortune in California. The brewmaster was a barrel-chested fellow, tall and fair with a wispy mustache and a booming voice, and he told tall tales he had overheard of the mobs rushing to find gold in California and the dark-eyed señoritas waiting with open arms in every doorway. Simon was immediately smitten, and vowed to follow him on the first available wagon train.

Conditions aboard ship were rudimentary at best. There was one toilet for every fifty people, and the drinking water was rank and bitter. The passengers jostled one another to receive their daily ration of thin soup, cabbage, and potatoes, and their blood ran cold seeing little children dying of hunger and exposure on the upper deck. There were rumors of cholera and dysentery spreading among the crew below decks. When the ship finally reached shore on September 4, a great shout of relief was heard, and the ragtag band of passengers, significantly diminished after the two-week ordeal, pushed and shoved to disembark.

True to his promise, Simon melted into the crowd with his newfound friend from Munich, giving his brother a friendly punch on the shoulder. "Come and see me in California!" he cried. "I'll have a fine house and horses and a beautiful wife by next year and you may change your mind and join me." But Mark concluded he'd had enough adventure and was ready to settle down to a quiet, hardworking life in the New World. Simon would eventually fail in his quest for gold and settle in Sacramento, where he married, had five daughters, and became the owner of a small neighborhood grocery store.

As Mark descended the gangway, the sweet, earthy aroma of produce in autumn struck him instantly—apples and carrots and cabbages. And it was no wonder, for the city marketplace was just a few steps from the harbor. It was noisy and thronged with people: butchers selling their hogs, girls carrying crates with squawking chickens, cheese makers, fishermen with their morning's catch. Dahlias and sunflowers and zinnias stood in milk pails at the flower stalls, just like at home. He was surprised to hear so much German being spoken and was startled by a tap on his shoulder. When he turned, he was confronted by his old friend Joseph Sachs with his pretty bride Sophia glowing beside him.

"Well, Mark, this is a surprise!" Joseph said. "I had no idea you were coming so soon. Have you been promised a job? A place to live?"

Mark, his cardboard suitcase with all his belongings still in hand, admitted he hadn't.

"It isn't so easy," Joseph continued. "I've been without work since we arrived. But maybe it will be different for you. You haven't any preconceived ideas about what you want to do with your life and seem content with whatever fate hands you. As for me, I've always wanted to be a teacher, and there are no openings here. However, I've just heard of an opportunity in Baltimore, which isn't so far away." Then he laughed. "Just like the old country," he said, "they find room for you when somebody dies.

"And speaking of rooms, my friend, if you haven't found a bed yet, perhaps you might consider taking our place at Frau Müller's boardinghouse. It is clean and cheap and convenient, and she keeps a German kitchen. You would only have to pay up the rest of the month's rent, which we owe, and the place is yours. Want to see it?"

The boardinghouse was nearby on North Street, and as they ambled through the Old City on this crisp, sunny morning, Mark marveled at the sights he saw along the way: rowhouses, with three-step stoops, taller than they were wide, one jammed right next to another; the Liberty Bell, the Free Quaker Meeting House, Independence Hall. The streets were straight, laid out in rectangles and paved with bricks—so different form the narrow alleys twisting through Bamberg, and the unmarked dirt paths they called streets in Trappstadt. In an area called Society Hill, a progressive Jewish congregation called the Knesset Israel, or KI, had been established by the synagogue just the year before. It was one of a number of German communities in the city that had established self-help societies and information centers for new arrivals. They spread the word about jobs and cheap farmland and organized social activities at which German-speaking immigrants could meet one another. It would be a good place to start looking for a job, Joseph advised Mark, whose name had been changed to Marcus by the immigration authorities upon his arrival in Philadelphia.

When they reached the boardinghouse, the Sachses led the way to the fourth floor. The room was small and sparsely furnished with a bed, a washstand, a rocking chair, and a small table. But it was spotlessly clean and had a lovely view over the neighboring rooftops to the river, and Sophia had made pretty flowered curtains and a bedspread. "It will look larger when we remove all our books," said Joseph, "and the price is right, three dollars a week." It seemed like heaven to Mark after the confinement he had experienced on board ship. Once his friends departed, he threw himself on the bed and slept until the next morning, when he met his new landlady, who was brewing coffee in the kitchen.

Frau Müller was a warm, motherly woman, with merry blue eyes and a braid of gray hair wound over each ear. Her son Manfred had a little shop on the ground floor facing the street where he sold yard goods and tobacco, but he had hopes of enlarging the business and peddling a wide range of goods from a horse-drawn wagon around the city. He was looking for a strong, reliable helper who could walk the streets seven days a week and would not be afraid to work, regardless of rain or snow or the humid summer heat. Mark jumped at the chance.

For the next three years, he traveled up and down High and Broad Streets, from the river to Eighth Street, with a horse and wagon, selling textiles and spices to housewives and learning the language and customs of his adopted land. Sometimes he would put in as many as fourteen hours a day. He was courteous, cheerful, and popular among his customers, particularly black people, whose problems he related to those of the Jews in Germany. And when he received permission from Frau Müller to plant a garden in the scrap of empty land behind the kitchen, he thought his happiness was complete.

Marcus paid lip service to the Sabbath at the Society Hill synagogue, sure that his mother would be disappointed if he didn't, and learned to play baseball, which was fast becoming the national sport, on Saturday afternoons. And on Sunday, there was always something happening at the synagogue—a picnic, a concert, perhaps a dance. In the letters he wrote to relatives in Germany, he always spoke of his good fortune and happiness. In America, no one had to pay "guardians" for protection, the judges did not show discrimination against Jews, and there were no unfair restrictions imposed on people of any faith. When she wrote back, his mother repeatedly asked when he planned to find a nice girl and get married.

In 1856, Ella's prayers were answered. Bertha Goldmann, a vivacious eighteen-year-old, came to the KI to meet some people of her own age. She and her parents, who were pipe tobacco importers, had emigrated from Bremen to New Orleans a few months earlier. Smart and ambitious, she did not find the laid-back lifestyle of the South to her liking and determined to go north and strike out on her own. She was a fine seamstress and quickly found employment in a milliner's shop, which had living accommodations on the second floor. She liked the tall, bearded young man who asked her to dance the first polka, and when he asked if he could see her again, she readily accepted. The next weekend, he came to call bearing a bunch of radishes he had grown in his garden. Bertha tucked them into the ribbon of her hat, and they went off for a stroll along the bank of the river. Six months later they were making plans for their wedding.

The newlyweds moved to a two-room flat on the fourth floor of 13 West North Street, in the Old City, and started planning for their future. By now, over a million Germans had immigrated to America, 140,000 from Bavaria, and many were choosing to settle in Pennsylvania, where there was an abundance of rich farmland and constant industrial expansion right in the heart of Philadelphia. As he hawked his wares along the river, Mark watched the newcomers arriving on steamships carrying all their worldly goods in small suitcases, and he recognized an enormous untapped market for sturdy, inexpensive clothing unfolding before his eyes.

Over dinner one night, Bertha told him she had seen a wonderful new invention being demonstrated downtown that day, a sewing machine. In less than ten minutes, the two agreed to gamble on their first investment. The next morning, Marcus applied at the First Bank of the United States for a $5 loan to buy one. He paid $2 down, promising to pay the rest in monthly installments at 5 percent interest. He used the balance of the loan to rent a storefront on busy High Street a few blocks from their home, where he started a new career as a tailor.

It was a happy time for the Goldmanns, who decided to anglicize their name by dropping an *n* when Mark became a naturalized citizen in 1853 and the clerk at the immigration office mistakenly registered him as Marcus. The tailoring business was successful, and their first child, a girl they named Rebecca, was born. That year,

Joseph and Sophia Sachs stopped by with their two young sons, Sam and Julius; they were moving again, this time to Boston. Marcus and Bertha tried to persuade them to stay and become partners in the business, but Joseph reiterated his passion for teaching. As they departed for "Yankee land" and a post at a posh private school, Sophia assured them they would always stay in touch and remain fast friends.

The Goldmans moved to larger quarters on nearby Castle Street and welcomed another daughter, Rosa, and in quick succession their first son, Julius, and twin girls. Louisa, the only survivor of the twins, was frail and tiny and demanded constant attention. When Henry was born a year later, she began to throw temper tantrums and would barely give the baby a glance.

Overall, the family turned out to be close and well behaved. Rebecca, a grave little girl who never strayed far from her mother's side, loved giving the babies their bottles and pushing them around the neighborhood in a buggy as if they were dolls. Rosa, a born actress, always "on stage" (as an infant, passersby called her "the smiling baby"), had a knack for making the infants laugh with her antics. Nothing gave her more pleasure than dressing up and playing games of "Let's Pretend" in which she could turn into a fairy princess, a member of a Turkish harem, or the Queen of the Nile whenever she felt like it.

Marcus's business quickly grew so large that he rented a store and began to sell clothing made by other craftsmen as well as his own bespoke tailoring. He invited his twenty-two-year-old sister Regina to come to America and lend a hand in the busy household and the shop. It was a happy arrangement until she met a merchant by the name of Ullman who had a small establishment down the street; she left to marry him two years later. It remained for Julius, a serious boy and an excellent student, to come in every day after school to mind the cash register and keep the books. Henry was eager to work in the store, too, but he had been slow learning to read and had repeated run-ins with tables and chairs in the house, which resulted in skinned knees and chipped pieces of china. It was finally determined that the youngster suffered from astigmatism, and his chores in the shop were limited to fetching and carrying articles from the storeroom or fastening the shutters at closing time. Bertha was convinced he would never succeed in a competitive world and was inclined to coddle and baby him.

They heard from Joe Sachs that he had moved again, this time back to Baltimore, where he'd been asked to start a private school. While there, Sophia also gave birth to twins, one of whom died at the age of five, but little Barney was robust and healthy and gave signs of being unusually intelligent. Marcus, meanwhile, was enjoying success beyond his wildest expectations. Over the next six years, the store thrived so well that he sold his sister's husband a partnership and moved to much larger quarters in a tonier location and opened a men's haberdashery.

But Philadelphia began to lose some of its steam as an economic center as the Civil War wound down. New York had replaced it as a commercial and cultural center, and money—making it, investing it, exchanging it—was the engine that was propelling its growth. Bertha had never liked the prudish provincialism in Philadelphia, and she prodded her husband to take his profits out of the store and relocate to New York, the city of progress, where opportunities seemed limitless. Marcus felt a twinge of disloyalty turning his back on the friendly community that had offered him safe harbor and his first steps on the ladder of success. Nevertheless, in 1869, exhibiting once more an extraordinary ability to reinvent himself and adapt to a new environment, a trait that would define his success over the years, he sold his share of the business and set out for new horizons.

CHAPTER TWO

Banking in "The Swamp"

*I*n 1869, gold was flowing into New York from California, and vast numbers of immigrants were arriving on ships from Europe almost every day, providing a potential clientele for bankers. At the time, no qualifications or special training were needed to enter the banking business. Following the example of established German-Jewish bankers like Joseph Seligman, who came from a similar background and had become very, very rich in a relatively short period of time, Marcus hung out a shingle advertising himself as "M. Goldman," a banker and broker of IOUs for the tanners and jewelers in the district known as "the Swamp" along Maiden Lane.[1] By buying promissory notes at a discount in the morning and selling them to banks in the afternoon, he enabled merchants to raise short-term working capital at attractive rates and, at the same time, to garner handsome commissions for himself. The notes, originally referred to as trade bills, later came to be known as commercial paper.

Marcus worked on his own from a tiny office in a basement next to a coal chute on Pine Street, with only an ancient part-time bookkeeper to help him.[2] Like others in the business, he conducted his business on foot, enabling him to develop new contacts and, at the same time, keep tabs on what the competition was doing. According to the custom of the day, he carried his commissions in the band of his tall black top hat for safety's sake.[3] Recalling his boyhood many years later, Henry Goldman told of coming home from school and seeing his father hail a horse-drawn buggy late in the afternoon and direct it to one or another of the banks uptown where he would exchange the day's paper. Then, after completing the negotiations, he would walk five miles to the family's cluttered apartment on the Lower East Side and join his family for dinner.

In spite of being a newcomer in the field, by the end of the first year Marcus was earning as much as $5 million. But privately he had even higher hopes and ambitions. His dream was to some day join the New York Stock Exchange, where far greater rewards could be realized by selling stocks and bonds. It is doubtful that he ever envisioned his business, successful though it became, as not just fulfilling his dreams but burgeoning into Wall Street's golden child, a firm paying each of its employees over half a million dollars in bonuses at year's end. More likely, he enjoyed the satisfaction of fashioning a financial bastion for his heirs and a means to afford them superior educations and a comfortable lifestyle that eschewed conspicuous consumption.

In all probability, the financial panic triggered by the 1873 collapse of Jay Cooke & Co., one of the top Philadelphia banking firms, proved somewhat of a windfall for Marcus. Jewelry and gemstones have historically been a financial safe haven in times of market disarray, and this collapse, caused by overspeculation in railroad stocks, was no exception. The escape to safety had a major impact on the wholesale jewelry market, which moved uptown from Maiden Lane to Forty-seventh Street west of Fifth Avenue, where it still flourishes today. Marcus, anxious to capitalize on every waking hour, moved in step with his customers and rented living space for the family in a brownstone right in the heart of the action. It was considered an upwardly mobile residential area, not far from the Astor residence. Bertha was delighted when she was given a carriage and a livery driver to make her daily rounds, along with a wardrobe befitting the wife of an up-and-coming financier.

Life at 4 West Forty-seventh Street straddled the old traditions of Germany and the driving energy that characterized the contemporary American way of life. For the most part, the Goldmans were a close-knit family who never forgot their German roots or their passionate loyalty to each other and their family heritage. The children were all bilingual and spent part of their summer vacations with their grandmother, who had moved into Aunt Bella's home in Bavaria after Wolf passed away. The only hitch in the harmonious family portrait they presented to the world was the tense relationship between Henry and Louisa, which occasionally erupted into floods of tears and noisy remonstrations. The boy was annoyed by Marcus's and Bertha's inclination to side with his doll-like sister in arguments and simmered with ill-concealed jealousy at what he perceived as their slights, real and imagined. He teased the girl unmercifully and put down every opinion she expressed. But she was a feisty youngster and not inclined to take a backseat to anyone, and she timed her tantrums well. Thus it often fell to Rebecca and Rosa, the older sisters, to quiet things down.

Henry and his brother Julius attended the Sachs Collegiate Institute for Boys on Fifty-ninth Street, founded and administered by the Goldmans' old friend Joseph Sachs, which was considered the city's number one boys' college preparatory school.[4] Sachs was a gifted teacher, but famously short on patience. He "would come down on you like a ton of bricks" if you were caught slacking, Henry remembered. Along with arithmetic, algebra, and geometry, the boys studied Latin, Greek, and German, physics, penmanship, read extensively in the classics, and frequently performed in plays and musicales.

Bright and precocious, Henry was an attentive listener who committed everything he heard in school—and much he overheard outside the classroom—to memory, achieving the high marks that German-Jewish fathers expected of their sons. He excelled at debating and was always among the first to volunteer opinions on any subject that came up for discussion. He was so nearsighted that he needed to wear thick lenses from the age of nine, and reading was a laborious task. No doubt impaired vision was a terrible burden for a boy who adored baseball but couldn't see well enough to catch a fly or hit a home run. He managed to escape the taunting and teasing generally dished out to the unathletic by helping his bigger, stronger classmates with their homework assignments.

On weekend afternoons, the whole Goldman family would go to Central Park, where they could watch the swells riding by in their stylish carriages, skate on the Fifty-ninth Street pond, listen to a band concert, or visit the monkeys and elephants at the zoo. Sometimes they ran into the Sachs family, Sam and Harry, Emelie and Barney, shepherded by fifteen-year-old Julius, who had been left in charge of his siblings and his father's school while Joseph was caring for an ailing Sophia in upstate Buttermilk Falls. Bertha, who was like an aunt to the young Sachses, would invite them to join the Goldman brood for Sunday dinner, insisting there was a large enough roast and chocolate cake for everyone. After the meal, the children would all gather around the prized new piano in the parlor, where Rebecca played old German folk songs and Rosa, often dressed in some exotic costume she had designed, led them in harmonizing at the top of their lungs. Young Julius Sachs was smitten with the girl, who was two years his senior, and upon reaching his majority, proposed marriage, with the eager endorsement of his parents and warm approbation of his in-laws-to-be.

Henry crammed hard for his preliminary college entrance exams, which he took at the Twenty-fourth Street YMCA when he was fourteen, and the following year passed his finals with flying colors. He was granted admission to Harvard, the college of choice for graduates of the Sachs school, and the place where his older brother was already studying pre-law. He knew how proud it made Marcus to see both his sons attending the oldest, most prestigious college in the land, where they would be part of the small group of elite Jewish students admitted.

He loved Cambridge, his rooms on Putnam Avenue, the atmosphere of dedicated intellectualism, the easy camaraderie and conversation between bright young minds brimming with ideas, the whole world of higher education. It was difficult to choose which of his studies excited him most—history, philosophy, literature, physics, music, history of art. His professors noted that he showed surprising insight in his papers for one so young and had a talent for expressing himself verbally. But by midterm of his freshman year, his eyesight had become so poor that he no longer felt capable of keeping up with his studies and he dropped out, leaving the world of academe forever. It was a bitter blow that fate had handed him, especially when he realized that his father's dreams for him would be shattered. Marcus, too straightforward to dissemble his disappointment, wondered out loud what kind of a career could be cobbled together for this son of his who had just turned seventeen. Wanting to ensure that he would have a comfortable livelihood in spite of his handicap, he contacted friends at the soft goods firm of D. Rosenberg and arranged for Henry to be hired as a clerk.

Whatever pricks of unhappiness he may have suffered were shelved two years later when Marcus was told that Bertha and Sophia Sachs had successfully arranged the betrothal of Louisa, the apple of his eye, to Rosa's brother-in-law Sam Sachs. It was high time for her to get married—she was twenty years old—and although Sam had failed to earn so much as a high school diploma, Marcus admired his selfless resolve in running a small dry goods business and shouldering the responsibility for his family's finances after the unexpected death of his father, who had been vacationing in Germany. The young fellow worked diligently and shared the ethical values Marcus himself held in such high regard, and what could have been more flattering than to have an acolyte who consulted him about every one of his decisions? Most satisfying of all was the comforting knowledge that his baby Louisa was totally taken with Sam.

In 1882 Henry, having shown business acumen beyond what was required in clerking, was offered a job as a traveling salesman by the firm of Dreyfuss, Willer, which was partially owned by the family of his sister Rebecca's husband, Ludwig. He held off giving his answer, hoping that instead his father might ask him to join M. Goldman, which by now was turning over $30 million a year and had accrued capital of over $100,000. With Marcus's sixtieth birthday approaching—and that was a landmark age in the nineteenth century—it seemed a logical time for him to be thinking of retirement, or at least reducing the stress of running the business single-handed.

The subject never came up. Julius and Rosa hosted a birthday party to which all the Sachs family members were invited, as well as the Goldmans. After the toasts had been offered, and the candles on the cake extinguished, Marcus asked for a moment of silence. He spoke of entering his twilight years, of the amazing turns in the road his life had taken since he left Germany thirty years before, and of his joy in being surrounded by such a wonderful family. And then he invited his son-in-law Sam to join him in the business. One side of the table looked stunned; the other beamed.

I've always believed that Henry was seen by his father as unable to manage such a role because of his physical ailments. While Marcus's decision was based on what he thought was common sense and not emotion, it was a crushing blow for Henry.

A year and a half passed, and Marcus was so pleased with Sam's performance that he asked him to become his partner. The offer, however, did not come gratis. Marcus said it would cost $25,000, which Sam could pay in three equal installments. However, after $5,000 had been tendered, when Sam and Louisa's third son, Walter, was born, Bertha insisted that the rest of the debt be forgiven. From then on, the firm was known as Goldman & Sachs.

Henry, still shocked that he had been passed over, was dumbfounded. By then he was in his middle twenties; he had shown brilliance in his brief attendance at Harvard, and though he had taken an unconventional path, he had made a good track record for himself professionally. He had always cherished what he perceived as a close relationship with his parents, and since Julius was engaged in the practice of law, he must certainly have anticipated that if anyone was going to be extended an invitation to join the firm, he would be the one. Did his father really favor Louisa that much? He sensed the beginning of his life was over and that the time had come for a whole new phase to begin. The following day he accepted an offer from a soft goods firm owned by his sister Rebecca's in-laws and became a traveling salesman of textiles, perhaps hoping to prove himself to his father.

It must have been a lonely life, traveling cross country in the 1870s, but it afforded Henry the time he needed for introspection and observation. The first transcontinental steam railroad had only been running for eight or nine years, and it did not incorporate most of the passenger amenities we have today. Dining cars were nonexistent, although pioneers like Fred Harvey were beginning to build restaurants and hotels and newsstands to replace the catch-as-catch-can facilities that had dotted the areas around the railroad stations in earlier days. Light bulbs were a newfangled invention with low wattage, making it difficult for someone with impaired vision to do a great deal of reading, and some of the lounge cars still used gas lamps. The telegraph had been crisscrossing the nation since 1859, but the telephone had yet to be invented, making it difficult to keep in touch with family and friends at home or to sustain any meaningful personal relationships.

Yet, as it turned out, the experience provided an education more valuably attuned to the times and prescient of the future than Harvard's hallowed halls. Henry was able to see beyond his reflection in the dark coach window and to gain a bird's-eye view of the mom-and-pop retailers, the little machine shops, the small-town banks popping up across the country. Perhaps he was already envisioning the expansion that would propel banking beyond their wildest dreams, and the innovative financial structures that would make them the building blocks of our future economy. At the same time, against the background of the clack-clack-clacking wheels carrying him from New York to Philadelphia, Boston, Chicago, and St. Louis, he was able to overhear the ramblings and rumblings of his fellow passengers, most of whom were also in trade, and to learn what people outside New York were thinking and talking about. Loneliness turned him inward, made him assess his strengths as well as his weaknesses, and turned him into a consummate observer. He banked those observations for use when the right moment came along.

Although he was an early riser, Henry would stay awake well past midnight, a habit that stayed with him his entire life. Night was the time when he could think most clearly. During those quiet, uninterrupted hours he could clarify his long-term goals and examine the equation linking the wanderlust of his own ambitions and the rationale that lay behind Marcus's appointing Sam to a partnership. He asked himself pragmatically, would the fates make room for him in the firm in the future? And if not, what were his other options? He thought of himself as the family's Joseph, exiled to the wilderness by his father, yet determined to come back some day and rise to greater heights than the rest of the family combined. And as he approached his thirties, there was a distinct feeling that something important was missing from his life: a partner to share his dreams, a sounding board for his passions, perhaps even romance.

Bertha was also becoming concerned about Henry's single status, and she was determined to find him a suitable bride. He still lived at home and had shown little interest in being a part of the social scene. He preferred visiting the new Metropolitan Museum of Art or the American Museum of Natural History or attending a musicale at the home of his parents' friends in the evening. Although he took vicarious pleasure in all the latest gossip, he was somewhat of a loner, comfortable with his own company, and reluctant to be pushed into an arranged marriage, which was still the norm among bourgeois Jewish-American families. His sister Rosa, whose home they were sharing at the time, tried to play matchmaker with several of her Sachs in-laws, but the linkups lacked chemistry, and Henry privately thought there were already enough Sachses mixed into the family.

The intellectual young women to whom he was introduced by his brother Julius, whom he respected and admired tremendously, impressed him with their talk of art and philosophy, but they failed to stir his heart.

Over the years, Marcus had maintained a personal friendship with one of his clients, a dry goods dealer from Hamburg, Isidor Kaufmann. Within ten years of his immigration from Germany, Kaufmann had become a naturalized citizen, paid off the debts on his little menswear shop, and made some judicious investments. He diversified his activities and began to manufacture ladies' wear in the bustling Grand Street neighborhood in Lower Manhattan. Combining sharp business acumen with a natural feel for fashion, his career as an entrepreneur took off like a rocket.

In 1870, Isidor had married Fanny Dobriner, and they had two charming daughters who, like the Goldman children, spanned the cultures of two continents. They spoke fluent German, immersed themselves in music and art, danced the waltz as if they had been brought up at the Hapsburg court, and were highly proficient in the everyday skills of keeping house, especially cooking and needlework. Babette, the eldest, had also inherited the organizational skills that contributed so much to her father's success, while her sister Rose was more of a tomboy and, though less beautiful, was very popular with the boys. The addition to the family circle of another baby girl, Florence, some twelve years later, prompted Isidor to commission Leopold Eidlitz, one of the most prominent architects in New York City, to build a new home for them, a stylish four-story brick-and-brownstone town house at 64 East Eightieth Street.

On Sundays, when they took their customary afternoon walks, Marcus and Bertha often stopped to observe how the house, a mile from their own home at Madison and Fifty-ninth Street, was progressing and to admire the elegant façade. When the construction was finished and the Kaufmans had settled in, Bertha suggested that they pay a courtesy call and leave their card on the salver in the vestibule. To their surprise and delight, Fanny, a lady totally lacking in pretense, answered the bell herself and invited them in to tea, which was served by eleven-year-old Babette. They were also introduced to the new baby, who was carried into the parlor for inspection by her adoring sister Rose, who was nine.

In 1885, Henry and Ludwig Dreyfuss were finally invited into the family fold, but only as junior partners. Dreyfuss, a likable, quiet fellow who lacked a great deal of drive, was one of the family that had employed Henry for the last three years, and hiring him was more of a payback than a matter of selectivity. The firm's name was changed to Goldman Sachs & Co., and from then on, for almost fifty years, all of Goldman Sachs's partners were members of the intermarried families.[5] Their assets, or a major portion of them, were tied up in the firm and provided working capital as well as savings. The practice continued until Goldman went public over a hundred years later, making it an extraordinarily profit-oriented organization. The partners were never allowed to withdraw any of their money without making a formal petition to the senior partners, which created a rather sticky situation from time to time. It made no difference whether the funds were needed for children's private school tuition or for second homes, yachts, or private Pullman cars

The original Goldman Sachs building at 43 Exchange Place

(the equivalent in those days of private jets), trips to exotic destinations, or divorce. Rules were rules, and there were no exceptions. This may have explained why Henry was in no hurry to move to a home of his own, even as he approached the age of thirty-three.

By now Babette had reached the age of seventeen. She was an enlightened young woman, determined, strong of will, and anxious to make a meaningful statement with her life. After she completed her formal education, she spent much of her time in charity work. She was a valued volunteer at the Henry Street Settlement, where she taught newly immigrated women how to adapt to the new world, and she raised funds to extend the outreach of the Visiting Nurses Association, which served the underprivileged and uninformed. Even at a young age, she was extremely persuasive and succeeded in gathering more than $10,000 for the VNA in six months' time.

It was her voice that first caught one's attention, a lilting, musical voice that always seemed to be concealing a little private joke. At five feet seven inches she was almost Henry's height, had curly brown hair, large gray eyes, and a marvelous complexion. Her real beauty would blossom as she matured. Somewhat of a flirt, she wasn't ready to settle down yet, and confided her impressions of the young men she met in a "Chap Book" she locked in the bottom drawer of her dresser. When she was introduced to Henry, she wrote that he was more a man of mystery than a prospect for romance. But the elder Goldmans and the Kaufmans, convinced that a good marriage was as desirable for the son of a tycoon as it was for a daughter of the "haute bourgeoisie," were persistent in bringing the two together, and, when pushed, Henry had to admit that he couldn't find any fault with Ba-

Henry and Babette Kaufman were married on January 21, 1890

bette. Heedless of a fifteen-year difference in their ages, they married seven months later.

January 21, 1890, was a lovely day for a wedding. It was unseasonably warm in New York in spite of a series of violent storms raging on the Atlantic that had battered steamships unmercifully with huge waves and hurricane-force winds. Russian influenza, which everyone called "the grippe," was sweeping the country. Nellie Bly had returned from her highly publicized trip around the world, and Sarah Bernhardt had received rave revues for her interpretation of Joan of Arc on Broadway. The *New York Times* breathlessly described the incredibly over-the-top flower-bedecked cotillion for five hundred guests at Mrs. William Astor's home as "one of the most brilliant social events of [the] season's social history."[6]

And in a show of their typical disdain for publicity, there was no announcement of the Goldmans' wedding in the rotogravures. One hundred fifty close friends and family were invited to the festivities, which were held in the gilt-and-plaster ballroom of the Kaufmanns' home. The groom was elegantly attired in white tie and tails, and the bride wore orange blossoms in her veil. Julius and Rosa Sachs's young son Ernest was the ring bearer, and he lost his plush toy dog during the ceremony, reducing him to muffled sobs and sniffles until it was retrieved at the end of the day. A coach and four white horses carried the newlyweds to the Brevoort House for their wedding night, and the following day they sailed for a month-long honeymoon in the Austrian Alps. Although the marriage started out as somewhat of a compromise for both of them, it ended up being much, much more.

CHAPTER THREE

The Goldmans and the Sachses

arcus Goldman had always considered an invitation to join the New York Stock Exchange the pinnacle of achievement. In 1896, when his firm's annual sales of commercial paper had doubled and the first Dow Jones Industrial Average was computed at 40.94,[1] he joined the magic circle of 1,100 members by purchasing a seat for $15,000. (More than a hundred years later, the price of a seat ballooned briefly to over $4 million.) Then he moved the office to 43 Exchange Place, where there was sufficient space for the five partners, ten clerks, and six messengers the firm employed. It had been a very good year indeed, punctuated by another landmark event, the fiftieth anniversary of his wedding to Bertha.

The children planned a festive celebration at the family summer home in Elberon, New Jersey, a beach resort an hour's train trip from Manhattan. It was known as the Jewish Newport at the turn of the century and the Hollywood of the East twenty years later when it was discovered by the theatrical crowd. Impressive Victorian and Italianate homes boasting immaculate emerald green lawns and luxuriant rose gardens overlooked broad Ocean Avenue, just steps away from a white sandy beach and the Atlantic Ocean. The Goldmans owned one of the most splendid of these, a twenty-four-room white stucco edifice with a red tile roof. Here Marcus's children had played as youngsters during summer vacations, and like half a dozen presidents of the United States and denizens of Wall Street, Marcus had chosen it as a retreat from the noisy bustle of the city. Because of the happy childhood memories with which they associated it, the children elected to stage their parents' golden anniversary party there, rather than at the posh new Hollywood Golf Club down the road.

On a warm day in June, the festivities were held in the garden, a strictly family affair, with just a few close friends like the Altschuls and the Gimbels and the Guggenheims, who also had homes in the vicinity, added to the guest list. A game of musical chairs had been set up for Robert and the little granddaughters—Florence, Bertha, Agnes, Hetty, and Ella, the only little girl among the Sachs children—who were all charmingly dressed in white organdy, ribbons, and lace. Sam and Louisa's son Arthur came down on the train from Harvard, and Julius Goldman's brilliant son traveled all the way from Texas, where he was involved in geological digs for one of the giant oil companies. (All of Julius's children were exceptional. Agnes became a renowned bacteriologist when she grew up, Hetty one of the century's outstanding Mesopotamian archaeologists, and Bertha a respected artist.) Little Henry Jr.—whom everyone called "Junie"—his long blond curls newly shorn, cuddled on his grandmother's lap until everyone was called to the table for lunch.

After the sumptuous meal was served—lobster bisque, Marcus's favorite rare roast beef, and a great assortment of vegetables freshly picked from the garden—two waitresses wearing black uniforms and frilly white caps carried in a huge chocolate cake and jeroboams of champagne. Julius, as the eldest son and toastmaster, rose and offered a tribute to his parents for giving the family their fine educations, happy home lives, and support for their chosen careers.

Family gathering in Elberon, New Jersey

Recalling his parents' modest beginnings in Philadelphia, he thanked them for the example they had set for their children by reaching for goals that others might have found impossible to achieve and by maintaining solid moral and ethical standards while making their dreams come true. He commended them for forging eternal bonds of love and respect between the siblings and for the grace and humility with which they conducted their daily lives. He concluded by quoting from Bertha's favorite poet, Goethe, "We are shaped and fashioned by what we love." The solemnity of the moment came to an abrupt halt when a Bedouin potato vendor swathed in colorful scarves appeared from the bamboo forest behind the house. Castanets clinking, she performed a suggestive Oriental dance in front of the startled guests of honor, then sank to the ground and removed her veils, one by one, revealing herself as none other than daughter

Rosa. A professional photographer had been engaged to memorialize the occasion, and there was much shuffling of places and smoothing of coiffures. When the portrait had been taken, a gift from all the children was carried out by two of the servants.

Babette was pleased that her sisters-in-law had asked her to help make the selection, but she was privately appalled at the choice. It was a large golden bowl, heavy and ornate, engraved with the names of every member of the family. It would have looked, she thought, more appropriate as an altarpiece in Temple Emanuel than a memento on the mantel of a family home. In her opinion, it was ostentatious and vulgar, the kind of thing that the social butterflies in Rhode Island might commission for their "cottages" and a far cry from the stylish art nouveau creations from Tiffany that she personally favored.

In later years this occasion would be remembered as one of the last times the Sachses and the Goldmans gathered on a social basis, laughing, reminiscing, and having a wonderful time. Who could have guessed that this close-knit, intermarried family would soon be enmeshed in a feud drenched in such animosity that the members and their children would not exchange a word for almost a hundred years?

Meanwhile, Henry bided his time, still playing a watchful waiting game. It wasn't until Marcus stepped aside two years later that he was elevated to the same level of authority as Samuel. When it did happen, he had just celebrated his forty-third birthday, and after years of being made aware that he was expected to fail, he was determined to achieve a role of leadership and dominance and prove all the predictions wrong.

It was hardly a cozy, *gemütlich* situation, but considering the circumstances, it was to be expected that a certain amount of friction would exist between the two brothers-in-law from the beginning. Henry understandably resented the fact that Marcus had loaned Samuel $25,000 to buy into the firm soon after his marriage to Louisa, and that the loan had later been forgiven. And while the Sachses enjoyed the comforts and pleasures of a privileged young married life, bearing four children and building up a cushy bank account over a ten-year period, Henry had for much of that time led the pedestrian life of a traveling salesman in the soft goods business, sleeping in boardinghouses, eating gray meat and overcooked vegetables with strangers or alone. When he married Babette, he was financially comfortable, but they were far from wealthy.

Sam, equally resentful for a different set of reasons, felt life had cheated him when economic circumstances triggered by his father's untimely death forced him to terminate his education before he graduated from high school. One can assume he bore a grudge against Henry, whom he thought had been given all the breaks but had failed to capitalize on them when he exited Harvard. He likely thought the younger man was spoiled and unjustifiably conceited.

There was no doubt that the new partners were polar opposites in almost every respect. They found it difficult to agree on anything except endorsing Marcus's dream of developing a financial partnership that would transcend dealing in commercial paper. Sam, reserved, conservative, and older by almost a decade, wore a coat and tie and high starched collar even in the middle of wilting August. Suspicious of everyone, wary, a worrywart, he was the very picture

of a turn-of-the-century banker. He was deferential to "the establishment" in society and finance; some called him a bit of a social
climber. He envisioned the Goldman Sachs of the future as an international banking concern and harbored ambitions to expand the
firm's currency dealings overseas. But in the meantime, between
1900 and 1910, he put all his energy into opening branch offices in
Chicago, Boston, St. Louis, and Philadelphia. Hard worker though
he may have been, he was never known to have an original streak.
But he was always the picture of loyalty, and he was determined to
preserve the firm's reputation and integrity, no matter what shocks
might rock the financial community.

Sam met his match in Henry, who was stubborn and immutable
in his convictions and could give as good as he got. No one, least of
all Marcus, was prepared for the fireworks that erupted when these
two divergent personalities clashed. Henry liked to work in braces
and shirt sleeves, a Havana cigar ever present in his hand. A creative, ambitious risk taker, his forte was trading railroad bonds,
which were the hottest commodity of the time. He proved to be an
extremely successful speculator, raising the partners' capital—and
his own—to $4.5 million between 1896 and 1904. As new busi-
nesses started up every day, and the distribution of agricultural and
manufactured goods was being revolutionized by the rapid spider-
webbing of railroads across the country, he was itching to get into
the action. But Sam shrank away from that plan, leaning toward
building the firm's financial future by expanding its contacts abroad.
His face would turn scarlet, and what the family referred to as "the
famous Sachs temper"[2] would erupt whenever the brothers-in-law

sat down to hash out their differences, for neither could ever admit that he was wrong.

In 1897, on one of his frequent trips to Europe seeking to expand Goldman's currency exchange business, Sam was introduced to Kleinwort & Sons, at that time one of London's most revered merchant banks. The senior Kleinwort partners were not only very rich, but high in the pecking order of British society, which impressed Sam enormously. The Kleinworts were recognized in London's "City" as financiers for the import of cotton from Egypt, sugar and cigars from Cuba, and coffee from Brazil and the Argentine, and they were eager to develop business in commercial credits and foreign exchange in America. With the British flush with cash and the Americans giving birth to one brand-new industry after another, a joint venture with them promised rich rewards for both parties. A collaboration was brokered and blessed by August Belmont, the Rothschilds' elderly, social, and immensely wealthy agent in New York, who vouched that "Goldman Sachs is one firm about whom nobody can say anything against."[3]

The Kleinwort relationship flourished and was mutually beneficial, with Goldman Sachs setting up a foreign exchange department to increase their bond arbitrage and commercial paper businesses and the Kleinworts providing letters of credit for companies, which was a new and very profitable addition to their services. However, it was in the field of lending money to developing businesses that both companies really made a killing. Kleinworts would become the underwriters for European sales of new issues brought to the market by Goldman, and Goldman was enabled to string together a continuing flow of successful new mega projects. All that, of course, came later and had an electrifying effect on the entire financial world.

In 1900, Marcus decided to retire and leave to Samuel the role of sole senior partner. A new bone of contention arose between the brothers-in-law when Samuel hired his brother Harry, who was exactly the same age as Henry, and his son Paul, newly graduated from Harvard, as brokers and shortly afterward elevated them to positions equal to Henry's as junior partners. Following fresh on their heels was another son, Arthur, and in 1906, Walter.

Henry, whose own children were ten, eight, and six years of age, was incensed. He viewed the imbalance of power and money between the two branches of the family as thoroughly unjust, a position to which he held fast until he was named senior partner and co-lead of the firm upon the reading of his father's will in 1904. It is ironic that Marcus wrote, in that last will and testament, "It is my earnest desire that after my decease, my children shall always live in such perfect harmony with each other as was the case during my lifetime, and shall ever be ready to comfort, mutually counsel and support, and if need be, to materially assist one another."

After Marcus passed away, all pretenses of brotherly love evaporated, and the partners no longer put on "street faces" to conceal their innermost feelings. When Henry accused Sam of being a tightwad because he never paid the boy from the neighborhood delicatessen who delivered their lunch, Sam responded that he only handled new bills; recycled money was dirty and full of germs.[4] At this, Henry would explode. When he remarked that Paul or Arthur did not have sufficient training to make sales calls, Sam's brow would darken and he would respond with a reminder that the Sachs boys were "*graduates* of Harvard." Henry was quick to retort that, in spite of his failure to earn a degree, he and six of his fellow class-mates had each donated $25,000 to fund a chair of Germanic art and culture at the university. The battles continued to rage.

From the moment of his arrival on the scene, five-foot-two-inch roly-poly Paul, whose true interest lay in the world of art rather than finance, was counting the days until he could amass enough capital to cash out and leave Wall Street, his pockets filled and his cultural aspirations free to take flight. In 1914 he began a distinguished ca-reer as a professor of fine arts and a curator at the Fogg Museum in Cambridge, Massachusetts. His wealth and business background opened doors to private collections for his students and opened checkbooks for new acquisitions. Among his impressive accom-plishments were the development of a celebrated course in museum curatorship and participation in the founding of the Museum of Modern Art in New York City. But during his association with Gold-man Sachs, traders and runners found him pompous and willful, and Henry called him "an irritating little bantam cock."

Arthur Sachs, according to family descendants, was a different cup of tea, described by relatives who remember him as "a very dif-ficult man," imperious, condescending, and inclined to fly off the han-dle at the drop of a hat. More than any of his siblings, he appears to have suffered from the attention deficit disorder that plagued many of the males in later generations of his family. Family members recall him as a cold and abusive parent, virtually shutting his children out of his life, sending them off to summer camp at the age of four and to boarding school when they were eight. For years he conducted a complicated three-cornered relationship with his first wife, the Bank of America heiress Alice Goldschmidt, and an impecunious French paramour, Georgette, whom he married when Alice died, reportedly of syphilis, at the age of forty-five.[5] He became a collector of impressionist art, founded a chair in French art at Harvard, and palled around with famous musicians of the era, such as the pianist-conductor Nadia Boulanger and composer Igor Stravinsky. When he relinquished the senior partner's seat after the end of World War I, it became clear that the lax oversight and reliance on the blandishments of others, such as Waddill Catchings, a well-known American economist, which gave him the opportunity to lead such a privileged life, was at the same time leading the firm to the brink of destruction.

While his nephews were involved in learning the ins and outs of finance, Henry expressed to his partners the conviction that underwriting railroad bonds was the road to the bank, and he was determined to follow it. The boom in railroad construction after the Civil War had transformed the country from an agrarian to an industrial economy and produced tremendous activity on Wall Street. Small-time investors were flocking to purchase attractively priced bonds with yeasty yields as the railroads turned to financial markets to raise funds for expansion. The Seligman family had become the first of the Jewish banking community to enter the railroad securities field, allying themselves with the prestigious House of Morgan and the all-powerful European Rothschilds in controlling the Pennsylvania Railroad; the Chicago, Milwaukee and St. Paul; the Baltimore and

Ohio; the Chesapeake and Ohio; the Denver and Rio Grande; the Gulf, Mobile and Northern; the Illinois Pacific; the Southern Pacific; the Texas and Pacific; and the Union Pacific. They were soon joined by Kuhn, Loeb & Co., whose youthful partner Jacob Schiff was fascinated by railroad development in all its ramifications and became determined that his firm would dominate the field.[6] Using the considerable resources of Kuhn, Loeb, he bought into the railroads, befriended the management, and became an expert counselor on the type of security that would best serve their long-term purposes. There was not a facet of railroad investment or operation that he did not carry in his head. When Henry approached these giants, who held a virtual lock on the business, to announce his intentions, they did not take kindly to this upstart's intrusion into their territory and made a counteroffer to buy out his railroad investments at cost plus 6 percent interest. In plain language, he wasn't welcome in their exclusive club.

Henry, always volatile and outspoken, was incensed, and minced no words about it. He insisted to Sam that Goldman Sachs should continue to pursue new railroad underwriting projects, especially west of the Mississippi. Sam, as usual, disagreed, arguing that he did not wish to tarnish the firm's good name or antagonize the major players of the day.[7] Henry's brother Julius, who was the firm's attorney, was called upon to settle the argument, and he opined that Sam's position made sense. Why stir the waters any further? Goldman Sachs should seek out other areas for new business and keep the peace.

The next day, Henry met his best friend, Philip Lehman, for lunch in the back room upstairs at Delmonico's, one of New York's most famous and elegant restaurants. Phil was the scion of a wealthy Alabama family that had made its fortune as cotton brokers and migrated north after the Civil War, settling in New York and becoming one of the founders of the Cotton Exchange. They had also founded a very successful bank. The Lehman name, on the Street, was synonymous with money.

Like Henry, Phil was an assertive, competitive personality, driven to achieve success in whatever he undertook. He had led Lehman Brothers into financing and developing the American Potash & Chemical Corporation, which they eventually sold at a huge profit to the Standard Oil Company of New Jersey. It was Phil who had first guided his family's firm into underwriting and into broadening their horizons to include merchant banking and trading securities on the stock exchange.

Henry and Phil lunched together often. As the sun streamed in through the lace-curtained windows, casting diamond-shaped shadows on the red and gold Axminster carpet, they ordered eggs Benedict, one of the restaurant's signature dishes, and chatted about their eleven-year-old children, Bobby Lehman, who was already an accomplished equestrian, and Florence, whose lush lyric soprano voice belied her years.

Dessert was offered—who could turn down the chocolate éclairs?—and their attention turned to their favorite subject: the market. They talked about the economic growth the world had been experiencing since the end of the "long depression" in 1897, the low unemployment figures in America, the increase in production, the protectionist tariffs abroad. And as they lit cigars over their coffee, they discussed the remarkable number of family-owned industrial and mercantile firms that were turning to Wall Street to raise capital for expansion. Henry observed that they represented a unique, untapped investment opportunity. What would Phil think about diverting some of the Lehman capital from commodity exchanges to underwriting issues for manufacturers and also the retailers who brought their products to market? It was a novel idea with huge upside potential that no one else had even thought of before.

The two considered setting up an underwriting firm of their own, Goldman & Lehman, but eventually decided to conduct business from their own firms as co-underwriters. Goldman Sachs would come up with the clients and Lehman the money, with the two sharing the profits fifty-fifty.[8] It was an opportunity for both firms to become full-fledged investment banks, and Phil was enthusiastic. When the waiter presented their bill, the agreement was sealed with a handshake. It lasted over twenty years.

The next step was to determine how to price the new securities. It was Henry's belief that retail stocks should be calculated by their earning power, the rate at which they turned over inventory and generated cash, rather than by their physical assets, like steel and railway shares.[9] This was an entirely new approach to financing commerce and probably the only way that start-up companies long on goodwill but short on material holdings could be marketed to an uninitiated public. It became known as the price/earnings ratio, and was determined by dividing the company's closing market price by its per-share earnings. Even today, it is the most widely used method for assessing the value of a security.[10]

Their first underwriting, the United Cigar Company, had been founded by a neighbor and friend of the Goldmans, Jacob Wertheim. Its origins were modest. At an early age, Wertheim had opened a tiny cigar store with his younger brother at Third Avenue and Fifty-fourth Street, where Jacob hand-rolled the cigars himself. The business thrived and grew, and additional workers were employed. Within fifteen years, a partnership was forged with the owners of three friendly competitors, Eddie Kerbs, Walter Schiffer, and the Hirschorn Brothers, all friends since their school days. Wertheim was the salesman and head of the firm, entrusted with turning over the product, Kerbs was the factory manager and tobacco buyer, and Schiffer the bookkeeper and accountant. The business grew rapidly, and after taking over several other tobacco firms they consolidated under the name of United Cigar Manufacturers.

In order to maintain their growth and popularity, it was clear that they would need money to build more factories and employ a larger sales force. Twenty million dollars was what they were looking for. When they came to Goldman Sachs for a bridge loan, Henry foresaw a perfect situation to test the viability of his new theory.

Marketing the shares took a little more time. A great deal of the preferred stock was sold in Europe through Kleinwort's offices and subsequently resold to American subscribers. Goldman and Lehman retained 25 percent of the common stock as a commission. For years the concern, which changed its name to the General Cigar Company, was the largest independent tobacco manufacturing company in the country. Interestingly, none of the Wertheim heirs became professionally involved in the business, but Jacob's son Maurice and

Henry's younger son Junie, who never became affiliated with Goldman Sachs, remained extremely close over the years. They attended the same school, belonged to the same Jersey Shore country club, and often dined as a foursome with their wives. Both were heavy smokers, but not of cigars, and died young. There are pictures in a family album of two-year-old Henry III and freckle-faced Jackie running about on the beach at Elberon in the "altogether" in the early Roosevelt years, when innocence still prevailed, and of the daughters and granddaughter of Kerbs, Schiffer, and Goldman competing with one another in horse shows.

Perhaps because of his own rocky road to becoming accepted as a member of his father's firm, Henry was always known to lend a sympathetic ear to people who had been turned down elsewhere as "losers." He believed in giving anyone with an innovative idea a chance to prove himself, even if he had flopped on other occasions; he was convinced that success can often be the godchild of failure. Consequently, when Julius Rosenwald, whom he had known since their teenage years, applied for a loan to enlarge Sears, Roebuck & Co., of which he was one-third owner, he found a sympathetic ear in Henry.

As a young bachelor, Julius had rented a room in the New York home of Sam Sachs's sister Emelia, who was married to Samuel Hammerslough, a well-known men's fashion retailer. Hammerslough was a native of Springfield, Illinois, and was fond of telling the story that he had custom-tailored trousers for the future president of the United States, Abraham Lincoln, who was so tall that he could never find trousers long enough to fit him. Hammerslough had a rather lukewarm opinion of Rosenwald, considering him "a nice young man who probably would never go very far." Most people agreed. They were less impressed with his talents than ever when the menswear manufacturing business Julius started with his brother failed, a victim of the recession of 1885. With help from a cousin, the two young men decided to try again, this time electing to make clothing in standardized sizes like the uniforms worn by soldiers during the Civil War. They chose to set up shop in Chicago, as it was closer to the rural population they thought would be their market.

The business thrived, and in 1891 Rosenwald married the daughter of Aaron Nussbaum, one of his chief competitors, and their companies merged. One of their biggest customers was the newly christened Sears, Roebuck Co., which had started out in the mail order watch business. Sears, who had a magnetic personality and an aptitude for writing colorful, persuasive copy, was well acquainted with the preferences and habits of the rural population who were on the Sears mailing list. Within seven years, he and his partner, Alvah Roebuck, who was the watchmaker, were producing an annual 332-page catalogue that they called "The Wish Book." It offered everything from fishing tackle and bicycles to stoves, guns, china, buggies, and women's clothing, and it reached 65 percent of the country's population. When Roebuck left the company because of ill heath, Richard Sears offered to sell his half of the company to Nussbaum and Rosenwald for $75,000, which they were able to raise with commercial paper brokered by Goldman Sachs.

Sears and Rosenwald proved to be a great team, Sears highly skilled in marketing and promotion, Rosenwald in management and sound business practices. They continued to diversify their product line, adding dry goods, consumer durables, drugs, hardware, furniture, and nearly anything else a farm household could require. Annual sales climbed from $750,000 to over $50 million.[11] The business expanded so fast that it soon outgrew its rented five-story building; within a year, it built or leased additional space in various areas of Chicago. Construction was started on a forty-acre, $5 million mail order plant and office building on Chicago's west side, which, with a million square feet of floor space, was the largest business building in the world. It was underwritten by $750,000 in commercial paper, although the retailer was only valued at $237,000 at the time.

In 1906, when the company's turnover was $50 million a year, Sears was convinced there were still more fields to conquer. Writing to a friend he said, "We do comparatively little business in cities, and we assume the cities are not at all our field. Maybe they are not, but I think it is our duty to prove it." And so they turned once again to Henry Goldman, who had supported their original effort, for a $5 million loan. But Henry had bigger ideas. He recommended selling shares on the open market, making it the first publicly owned retail operation, or IPO, in the world while simultaneously collecting huge commissions for his firm.

The establishment Wall Street houses had hardly recognized manufacturers, let alone the retailing sector, as appropriate offerings, feeling that even Goodyear Tire & Rubber and Edison Storage Battery Co. were far too speculative. They sniffed and turned up their noses and laughed behind their well-manicured hands. Sam

Sachs was one of the hardest sells at the beginning, reluctant to endorse what he considered an overly risky endeavor. His voice reached a shrill pitch as he argued against Henry's proposal, and only after Alexander Kleinwort stepped in to convince him of the immense rewards in sight if the issue was successful did he agree to the firm's participation. Over the next few months, the underwriters sold the 7 percent preferred shares to the public for $90 a share, retaining the $50 common for themselves—"More money than Richard Sears ever thought it would be worth," according to Sam's son Walter. The gamble doubled the firm's investment, netting a $10 million profit, and turned both Goldman Sachs and Sears into household names. And the lifestyle of the Goldman family became plushier and more social, as well as more philanthropically inclined.

Babette immersed herself in charity work, notably for the United Hebrew Fund, Mount Sinai Hospital, and social services for deaf and crippled children, which had been favored beneficiaries of her father-in-law. She was a persuasive fund-raiser and was respected for her taste and imagination in planning flower shows, art exhibits, and elegant musicales, which garnered significant funds for her chosen causes. Admiring her style and beauty, society artists and photographers vied to portray her.

Like many of her contemporaries, she delegated the major responsibilities of child care to an efficient fräulein and a staff of German servants. Thus it fell to Florence, the eldest of the Goldman children and on the brink of puberty, to assume a maternal role in the family, particularly in relation to her younger brother, Junie, who from the time he was wearing long curls was periodically confined to the house with severe earaches. When he was diagnosed with mastoiditis at the age of eight, it was she who accompanied him to the hospital for the delicate emergency surgery. And when the older boy, Robert, failed to show up for dancing school or his piano lessons, she would shield him from their father's explosions and make up fanciful cover stories. A tall, plump girl with a Grecian nose, wavy blond hair and a complexion as lovely as her mother's, Florence played tennis, liked to collect miniature antique furniture, and shared her parents' love of music. At an early age she was a devotee of Steuben crystal, Cartier, the lovely colors and fabrics of Madame Worth gowns from Paris, and, like her papa, chocolate. Of all the children, she shared the closest relationship with her mother, although it was plain to see that Robert, with his infectious grin and flashingly handsome looks, was Babette's favorite.

Unlike Henry and Babette, who assumed such a hands-off approach to child rearing, Sam and Louisa were extremely ambitious for their offspring and controlled all their activities and decisions. Their youngest child and only daughter, Ella, very pretty, very bright, was treated like a china doll and, unlike other little girls on Murray Hill, was never allowed out of the house without the supervision of her British governess. Walter, the youngest son, recalled many years later the French conversation lessons to which his parents subjected him three times a week at the end of the school day, when he really wanted to be out playing baseball with his classmates. There was no

The Goldman children, Florence, Robert, and Junie, with their fräulein

questioning which university he would attend; it had to be Harvard. Once there, he was a big man on campus, proud of his position on the staff of the *Harvard Crimson,* and a classmate of Franklin Delano Roosevelt. Apparently singled out as Sam's heir apparent while he was still in his early teens, he accompanied his father on business trips to Europe and London, dined at the Kleinworts' palatial home (where he embarrassed Sam mightily by shaking hands with the butler, mistaking him for one of the family because he was wearing "soup and fish"), and, upon graduation from college, was apprenticed successively to French, German, and British banks, where he learned the ins and outs of arbitrage.

CHAPTER FOUR

Going Public

*W*alter's father had promised to treat him to a trip around the world on his way home at the end of two years in Europe, but in 1907 the first of the twentieth century's panics occurred, and he was summoned home to go to work. In the previous ten years there had been a dramatic increase in the number of small investors in the market, and a shift in interest from bonds to stocks. Everyone wanted to get in on the action on Wall Street, where the easy money lay. Banks were chock-full of deposits, and consumers were on a seemingly endless spending spree. And then a speculator by the name of F. Augustus Heinze sold his shares in Montana copper mines for $16 million, moved to New York, bought the Knickerbocker Trust Company, and became director of a national financial chain. His aim was to forge consolidations and, eventually, corner the copper market.

Knickerbocker, which included business and society luminaries among its officers and directors, had recently relocated to 234 Fifth Avenue, next to the elegant new Waldorf Astoria Hotel (now the site of the Empire State Building). The move was intended to serve "uptown" residents and relieve them of having to travel to the financial district to conduct their banking affairs. It was one of a number of trust companies vying with banks for control of the nation's money by offering higher interest rates and sidestepping laws requiring they maintain large cash reserves like ordinary banks. From its charter in 1884 until the panic, it was considered eminently successful and among the most trusted fiduciaries in the city. While its primary business was to act as trustee for wealthy individuals, corporations, estates, and court funds, it also issued interest-bearing certificates of deposit and offered checking facilities. The press reported that its capital was intact and secure.

But there was a dirty little secret in the back rooms of Knickerbocker. Heinze, his brother Otto, and the bank president, Charles T. Barney, had been speculating with the depositors' funds in an attempt to corner the market in United Copper shares, and their manipulation had fallen on its face. The National Bank of Commerce warned Barney that it would stop accepting Knickerbocker checks unless he made immediate restitution, which he could not do. Government bonds at the time had to be deposited with the Treasury in order to obtain banknotes, and the supply of government bonds at Knickerbocker was insufficient to cover a depositors' run on the bank.

Panic occurred when the public got wind of the situation, a panic that threatened not only Wall Street, but also the entire financial fabric of the city and the nation itself. Money had simply dried up. Crowds mobbed Knickerbocker's iron doors on Fifth Avenue, loudly demanding their money back. A sharp observer might have spotted a street-smart fifteen-year-old from Brooklyn named Sidney Weinberg mixing with the crowd, soliciting five-dollar tips to hold places in line for dozens of anxious depositors waiting to recoup their money.

According to author John Steele Gordon in *An Empire of Wealth: The Epic History of American Economic Power,* more than $8 million was withdrawn in less than four hours, and the panic quickly spread from one bank to another. Knickerbocker's funds were completely wiped out in forty-eight hours, and the resulting domino effect culminated in a nationwide depletion of liquid cash and a 48 percent drop in the New York Stock Exchange, which took almost five months to return to its previous level. The least fortunate depositors were left with valueless paper deposits, and the disgraced Barney shot himself several weeks later. Some of the bank's outstanding depositors committed suicide as well.

J. P. Morgan, whose firm was still the dominating force in the money markets, was called upon for emergency assistance. He assembled a group of banking experts to examine the assets of doubtful institutions and determine which were still sound and worth saving. Knickerbocker, unable to come up with sufficient funds to fulfill the demands of its depositors, did not pass the test.

In the days before the establishment of the Federal Reserve System in 1913, ordinary banks were required to maintain large cash reserves, but trust companies were not. Nor did the trusts subscribe, or wish to subscribe, to any organization such as the Clearing House, which acted as something of a bulwark against disaster. As stock market prices retreated at an alarming rate, industrial activity came to a screeching halt, and brokerage houses teetered on the brink of bankruptcy. Cash for loans was nonexistent. Morgan called upon the U.S. secretary of the treasury for help to stabilize the exchange and some of the weaker banks, which he agreed to do, although he stopped short of bolstering the trusts.

The largest and least transparent of the shaky institutions was the Trust Company of America, which had held a large block of stock in Knickerbocker as collateral for loans and was rumored to be connected with Heinze's copper speculations. Under pressure from Morgan, the treasury secretary permitted banks to lend money to the trust companies if they in turn would lend it to the Trust Company of America. A $10 million fund was raised, but that was far from the end of the trouble. The stock exchange floundered and the panic spread.

Morgan summoned the presidents of New York's leading banks to his office and told them that $25 million more must be raised immediately to keep the exchange from closing down entirely. The sum, however, proved to be a stopgap measure. Soon he had to requisition an additional $15 million. As the world watched, some of the larger brokerage houses rocketed toward bankruptcy. Morgan turned in desperation to John D. Rockefeller, titan of the oil industry, to join him in establishing a $40 million fund to rescue the trusts, but Rockefeller turned him down.

To further the troubles, European investors were reluctant to buy New York City's bonds under the circumstances, and the mayor desperately appealed once again to Morgan for help, which he personally agreed to provide after extracting a number of protective measures, including a bankers' committee to oversee the city's accounting problems. He summoned over one hundred of the city's leading bankers and trust officers to his private library and reportedly locked them in overnight while they hammered out a way to redirect money between the banks and secured international lines of credit with which to rescue the weaker trusts. The result was a bailout of the Trust Company of America and another troubled institution, the Lincoln Trust. Knickerbocker was again left out in the cold.

Morgan's heavy investment and decisive actions saved the day, but his moves were controversial and hardly considered philanthropic. He had underwritten the loan to the trusts at 6 percent interest, and this ultimately resulted in vast quantities of capital falling into the hands of a select group of moneymen, while consolidating Morgan's grip on competitive companies and, ultimately, the entire steel industry.

Henry Goldman, who had not been invited to participate in the meeting because Morgan still considered him an upstart and an outsider, refused to believe Knickerbocker was a dead issue; he viewed it instead as an opportunity. Feeling that the trust had received a thumbs-down largely because of Heinze's and Barney's disreputable characters—the institution still carried masses of commercial paper that had yet to come due—he persuaded friends at the solvent Columbia Trust, acting as white knights, to step in and absorb Knickerbocker's assets and restore its stability. It was a good bet. Columbia merged with the aggressive Irving Trust Company ten years later, and Henry became a member of the board of governors. Nearly a century of glowing profitability passed before it was taken over by the Bank of America.

Following the panic, there was a shift in the public's investing sentiment from bonds to stocks, and speculation became a significant part of the American culture. Its prevalence made it increasingly apparent that major banking and currency reforms were required to save the citizens from themselves. Such unlikely allies as Morgan; William G. McAdoo, who would later become secretary of the treasury under President Woodrow Wilson; and Henry Goldman, representing Goldman Sachs, were among the Wall Street heavyweights who advocated a central bank that would provide the country with a more secure, more elastic, and more stable economic and financial structure, one that would assure banks the ability to obtain currency ensuring the security of their short-term assets.

In order to push the government into acting swiftly, Henry turned to an old friend, Henry Morgenthau Sr., a New York real estate tycoon, for an introduction to Wilson, who was the Democratic candidate for president in 1912. After a lifetime of voting for the Republican Party, Henry had become so fed up with Teddy Roosevelt's left-wing trust-busting crusade against big business, which he felt had backfired disastrously, that he had switched parties and become a heavy contributor to Wilson's campaign. Nearly a year before the election, in which Wilson scored a landslide victory among the delegates but won only 42 percent of the popular vote, Henry wrote the president-elect an eight-page letter, on which Wilson's personal secretary had handwritten "For immediate attention," warning of economic difficulties ahead unless Congress acted quickly to reduce the threat of evaporating credit. He pointed out that all the great commercial nations of the day were supported by some form of central bank and that since 1873 none of them had experienced a panic. The business of banking was basically the buying and selling of debts, he observed, but under current conditions American institutions were only permitted to operate on the buying side since there was no market in which they could sell. This signaled the possibility of a good deal of speculation, which would result in the banks' reaching their reserve limits and being unable to function. This in turn would result in either a "barbarously high money market unknown in other civilized countries or panic with all its endless misery." He offered the president his services in any way he might find helpful before sailing for "a much needed six-month vacation in Europe."

Wilson valued Henry's counsel and pushed Congress in 1913 to pass the Federal Reserve Act, which would provide a means to control the money markets of the country by linking the federal government with the existing private banking system. The act created a central institution consisting of a national system of banks, and entrusted it to act as fiscal agents of the Treasury and enabled it to establish new reserve requirements, regulate the nation's money supply, and protect the nation against future liquidity crises. The primary bank, established in New York, rediscounted to eight satellite banks spread out between the two coasts, following the model of London banks dealing with the Bank of England. With the exception of rural bankers, who felt their interests had been pushed aside, the public generally felt reassured by the formation of the Fed, as the Federal Reserve System came to be known. But they didn't know quite what to think about a corollary agency, the Internal Revenue Service, whose sole purpose was to collect taxes dedicated to paying interest on the public debts of the government of the United States. This had *not* been one of Henry's proposals.

Henry's honeymoon with the Democratic Party did not last long. He disparaged Wilson's "utter lack of foresight in maintaining American commercial rights" and "ill-considered labor legislation," which supported trade unions and antitrust action. He was outraged by the president's "vacillating foreign policy in Mexico." Before his election Wilson had opposed the imperial policies of Teddy Roosevelt, who wanted the United States to forcefully spread democracy throughout the world, and had supported the right of the Mexican people to choose their own government, but after the election Wilson had done a complete about-face and dispatched American troops south of the border to defeat Pancho Villa's counterrevolutionaries. It did not take Henry long to reverse course politically again, and in 1916 he threw his support behind Charles Evans Hughes, and for the rest of his life voted Republican.

Meanwhile, the global economy was growing at an impressive rate, tariffs were raised, and America ushered in an era of new products that were destined to transform the way people lived. Goldman Sachs, Lehman, and Kleinwort's had underwritten the Underwood Typewriter Company and B. F. Goodrich, the tire and rubber manufacturers, in rapid succession. And then Henry was brought a letter of introduction by a youthful entrepreneur from Denver.

David May was a classic example of the Horatio Alger protagonist who appealed so much to Henry. As a young man, May had sought his fortune mining for silver in Leadville, Colorado, only to come up empty-handed. He had then packed up whatever savings he had been able to salvage and invested them in the Great Western Auction House and Clothing Store, where he sold flannel long johns and copper-riveted Levi's to the local prospectors. He enjoyed the work and the person-to-person contact, and the venture flourished. In 1890 he opened a clothing store in Denver, which was also a success. Two years later he pushed eastward, opening the Famous Barr Emporium in St. Louis and, a few years later, in Cleveland, the first store to bear his name.

By 1912 May's ambitions had grown, and he envisioned a chain of nationwide retail establishments. But it was clear that a large infusion of cash was needed to rent the real estate, build the stores, and purchase the enormous quantity of merchandise that was required. He was less than confident of the reception he might receive at Goldman Sachs. Upon his arrival, he was greeted by a fellow in shirtsleeves sitting at the desk near the doorway, smoking a big cigar and reading the *New York Times,* whose front page was emblazoned with a headline reporting that the transatlantic liner *Titanic* had struck an iceberg and sunk, losing over 1,200 lives at sea. While waiting to see Mr. Goldman, May and this friendly person whom he assumed to be a clerk discussed the tragic occurrence. A half hour passed, and May went on enthusiastically about the project that had brought him to Goldman Sachs and what great opportunities it would open up to the investment house. How embarrassing it must have been when he discovered that he had been boasting about himself to one to the cleverest underwriters on the Street!

Henry immediately saw the huge potential of gathering a number of retailers under one name, pooling their purchasing power, and implementing a cooperative marketing push across the country. He recognized it as a landmark approach to modern marketing that would benefit the consumer as well as the investor and agreed to float the issue. Soon the names of famous department stores owned and operated by the May family were strung like Christmas lights across the country: Filene's, famous for its bargain basement; Marshall Field's, with its branches throughout the Midwest; L. W. Ayres; and Kaufmann's. Even the discount Target stores so popular with thrifty shoppers in the early part of the twenty-first century were a spin-off division. May was acquired by Federated Department Stores in 2005 for a cool $11 billion in stock. Henry's 1937 obituary reported that he owned over five thousand shares prior to a number of stock splits that followed.

Even May seemed like small potatoes compared with F. W. Woolworth, which entered the *Guinness Book of World Records* a hundred years later as the largest department sore chain in the world. When their management went shopping for an underwriter to consolidate and market their 596 stores, Goldman Sachs was a logical choice. Frank Woolworth appeared to have been born with the marketing savvy and innate ambition that Henry considered key to success. The son of a farmer, he started working in a dry goods store in Watertown, New York, near the Canadian border, and drew no salary for the first three months because the owner didn't feel he deserved one while he was learning the business. Over the next six years, while he was assigned one menial task after another in the shop, he noticed that at the end of the day leftover items were removed from the shelves, marked down to five cents and placed on an open table marked "clearance." He expanded on the idea, borrowing $300 to open his own store, where every one of the items was priced at five cents to begin with. It was a quick and resounding flop.

But Woolworth didn't give up on his idea, and in 1879 he opened a second store in Lancaster, Pennsylvania, in which all the merchandise was priced at ten cents. His concept was to purchase goods directly from manufacturers and sell them to the public at fixed, discounted prices, undercutting the offerings of local merchants. He displayed everything so that customers could make a selection for themselves, eliminating the need for a clerk to fetch and carry stock from behind the counter to answer all their shopping needs. The operation was cost and time effective, and the Lancaster store succeeded. Frank took in his original employer and his brother as partners and proceeded to open a large chain of stores across the country, frequently teaming up with friendly rivals. In 1912, when Woolworth's became a publicly traded company, the synonym for "five-and-tens," they were recognized as one of the hottest commercial phenomena of the twentieth century.

Henry's younger son, Junie, was one of Woolworth's typical customers when he was a boy. He liked to browse the Woolworth aisles with his friends Willie Kraus and Bob Scholle on Saturdays, purchasing school supplies and candy and detective stories and winding up at the fountain for an egg cream or a Broadway soda. A popular fellow who did well in his studies and enjoyed playing tennis and baseball, he was a jazz buff who played the mandolin almost as well as a professional. His two passions were his motorboat, which his parents had given him on his fourteenth birthday, and the New York Stock Exchange. There was never a question about whether he would follow his famous father onto the Street. It was more a matter of when.

When his mother was preparing for his sister Florence's December wedding to Edwin Vogel, a young lawyer from a prominent New York family, and his brother Robert went off to Williams College, Junie looked forward to one-on-one time with his father and anticipated closer rapport. Henry's stories about the companies the firm was taking public fired his imagination as much as his favorite Kipling novels and Junie relished the thought of sharing the triumphs and tribulations he had experienced at school with him. But Henry had a new love: collecting significant works of Flemish and Renaissance art. He had met the charismatic dealer Joseph Duveen on one of his frequent sailings to Europe and purchased a phenomenal Rembrandt portrait that had never before been on public display. Now his passion for surrounding himself with the most beautiful art in the world far outstripped any parental interest he might have had in the mundane activities of a schoolboy. With the underwriting of the Studebaker automobile company on the horizon, Junie was hustled off to Hotchkiss School, the snooty boys' preparatory school as well known for its anti-Semitic student body as its educational standards. The cool reception he received there may have put the final nail in the coffin of the Goldman allegiance to Judaism, which with the passage of time had become more of a casual association than a religious conviction.

Henry was excited by the prospect of launching the first public issue of an automobile manufacturer. He had no doubt that it would be one of the top issues ever brought out by Goldman Sachs. Even

Goldman Sachs issued stock in Studebaker, the first automobile manufacturer to go public

his contentious in-laws recognized this as a landmark in the firm's drive to the top. The automobile, one of the greatest influences on the American lifestyle, had captivated the public since 1903, when Henry Ford produced his first Model A. His Model T, first produced in 1908, eclipsed the sales of Olds and Cadillac and Buick, and Ford was approached to become part of the nascent General Motors Corporation in 1908, but the deal fell through when the New York banking community refused to provide up-front financing to cement the deal. While Ford failed to become part of the combination, it had given Studebaker's introduction of their first models a terrific boost.

The company was founded by four brothers, Henry, Clem, Peter, and John Mohler Studebaker, who had migrated to California in the

1850s to make wheelbarrows for miners during the gold rush. When they returned to the Midwest six years later, they invested their earnings in the manufacture of Conestoga wagons, which were widely used in settling the American West. They were extremely successful and became one of the largest wagon manufacturers in the world, supplying the United States Army, among others, throughout the Civil War. By the 1880s, their sales had soared above $2 million and production topped 75,000 units. Theirs was the only company in the business to switch from horse-drawn to electric-powered vehicles, and just two years later they introduced gasoline-powered cars. Sales and net profits multiplied rapidly—ironically, the general consensus was that "cheap American production" was responsible— and the stock issue, just as Henry had predicted, was a bang-up success.

As a member of Studebaker's first board of directors, Henry felt personally responsible for upholding the company's moral and ethical standards in its day-to-day operations. He helped to create a socially responsible company that championed liberal labor policies and considered capital, management, and labor to be mutual partners, each fundamental to the health of the business. The company offered salaries above market rates and instituted a profit-sharing plan for management and a wage dividend for labor, and they adopted stock purchase and pension plans and granted vacations with pay to factory employees. These were groundbreaking ideas and way ahead of their time. If one fast-forwards to the present day, the philosophy is echoed to a large degree by Goldman Sachs's amazingly generous across-the-board year-end rewards to its vast corps of employees, and the philanthropic outreach that is a cornerstone of its culture.

With the expansion of the Goodrich Tire & Rubber Company in 1912 and subsequently the founding of the CIT Financial Corporation, which joined Studebaker's four thousand dealerships in providing financing to car buyers and created a vast new pool of customers, Goldman Sachs was on a roll. No one questioned the fact that Henry was the creative visionary driving the money machine, the most influential partner, and if there were rumors that Goldman had a new industrial issue on the horizon, it was often completely sold out even before a price was established.

Things were less sanguine on the home front. Robert, the Goldmans' tall, dark, and handsome twenty-year-old son, was giving both of his parents considerably less joy. While still an undergraduate at Williams, he had met and fallen in love with a young woman named Edith Ostend who was playing a bit part on Broadway in a bedroom farce, *The Belle of Bond Street*. After a very short romance, they were secretly married in Jersey City and set up housekeeping in a little apartment on West Ninth Street in Greenwich Village. Come September, when the fall semester was scheduled to begin, they planned that Robert would continue with his studies, assuming that he would be handed a partnership at Goldman Sachs when he graduated. Edith was going to take the train to Williamstown on Friday nights and sneak into Robert's dormitory through a bay window on the ground floor, flouting all rules that forbade women to set foot on the hallowed campus. Henry and Babette were blissfully unaware of the arrangement. They had departed for Europe around the time of the nuptials and were focused on banking affairs abroad and celebrating the birth of their first grandchild, Betsy Vogel, in Paris.

So autumn came, and with it Labor Day, and school, unhappily, beckoned. The summer holidays, with carefree days at the beach and weekends under a mountain moon, came to an end. Robert, his head in the clouds, was making C's and incompletes in his studies and trying to keep his clandestine marriage a secret from the Williams authorities when Chester Mann, Henry's private secretary, who also lived in Greenwich Village, spotted the young couple entering their love nest over the Columbus Day holiday. The cat was out of the bag.

A few days later, Mann and three detectives were dispatched by Henry to the house on Ninth Street around nine in the evening. Mann slipped through the unlocked front door and the detectives ran up the fire escape, surprising Edith and a friend, who introduced himself as Nathan Harris. Edith looked very fetching in bloomers, a combination suit, and a petticoat, and Harris was in the process of removing his coat and shoes when the unexpected guests arrived. Both were sipping vintage champagne. Edith was nonchalant about the whole affair and offered all the gentlemen a drink. She was chatty and quite agreeable to signing a sworn confession to her state of dishabille, confident that her infidelity case would be settled out of court and she would no longer have to work for "twenty two per." Less than two weeks later, she was caught in another raid, this time at the Hotel Wellington in Chicago, in the suite of a man named Lambert whose hotel bill was being charged to her. She vehemently declared that she had been "framed up," saying that she had only been in the room for two minutes before the break-in.[1]

Henry would have no more of "this nonsense." He disregarded Babette's entreaties, and Robert was not given another chance. Henry's dream had been to establish a dynasty of his own at Goldman Sachs, one that paralleled the Sachses, but there was no room for dissembling at the top of the firm, and Henry was unyielding in his decision. His plans for succession would simply have to wait until young Junie matured. Before the Williams authorities were able to lower the ax, Henry told Robert to pack his bags and sent him to Montana, where he worked as a ranch hand for $40 a month for the rest of the year.

As guardian for his underage son, Henry sued Edith for divorce in New York Supreme Court.[2] Included in the evidence presented to the jury were two telegrams requesting money, claiming that the bride was starving. One was addressed to a Nathan Harris in Newark, New Jersey, and another to Charles E. Fisher of Manhattan. Mr. Fisher testified that he had hocked Edith's wedding ring for $437 in order to obtain the money. Although he claimed that he had never used any endearing terms toward her, a letter dated just a few weeks earlier was produced in which he addressed her as "Dear Honey Girl" and assorted other endearments. Robert's testimony was brief; he was not permitted to identify a package of love letters he had written to his wife, the judge ruling they were too "provocative" to read in public.

Edith, smiling sweetly and delivering her testimony with breezy confidence, countersued her father-in-law for alienation of her husband's affections.[3] The judge awarded her ten dollars a week alimony and one hundred dollars in attorney's fees. It was just the first of Robert's four divorces and unquestionably the least expensive.

Around the office, young Walter Sachs, the newest family recruit to the firm, now became somewhat of a surrogate son to Henry. Walter was twenty-three when he started at Goldman Sachs, and, of all the Sachses, Henry had the greatest rapport with the personable youngster and found him good company. Walter had always been intrigued by the world of finance, but Sam considered him too young to work in the firm when he graduated from Harvard, and so he was enrolled for a year in the law school at Cambridge. He came to the firm in 1908, just after the panic ended, and spent his first week with his older brother, Arthur, "going around visiting New York banks and seeing how we sold the paper to banks, merchants' paper. . . . It was the original business that my grandfather was in, in 1869 before we got into international banking and the security business," he recalled in his oral history.[4] On Monday of the second week, he was let loose on his own to solicit business from banks in Hartford, Connecticut. His initial attempts were a total failure, and he was even dressed down by one of the major accounts to whom he had been dispatched for not being very well informed about the company whose paper he was trying to sell.

Things began to look up after a year or so, when his father gave him the opportunity to make a swing around the country and introduce himself in major cities. Chicago was one of his early stops, and the first man he called on was J. Ogden Armour of Armour & Co.,[5] to whom he sold almost half a million dollars in sterling credits, which were drafts sold on discount in the London money market that produced cheaper currency than American bills. Armour, a warm and friendly man, had not been a client of Goldman Sachs before, and Walter was, of course, elated—"cock of the walk," he called his euphoric self in his oral history.[6] Many years later, when he called on Armour again, he told him, "I've never forgotten that [you were] so nice to a young neophyte like me . . . and gave me the most tremendous lift I'd ever had in my early business life."[7]

By the time Walter was broken in, securities far outpaced commercial paper in his sales portfolio. When he returned from his travels, he was inclined to draw a chair up to his Uncle Henry's desk and describe his stumbles and successes on the road. It put Henry in mind of his own youth and made him eager for his son Junie to grow up and begin to be part of the firm.

One of Walter's fondest recollections was of a call he made on the chief officer of Drexel and Company, whom he'd grown to really like. In 1909, the syndicate of which Goldman was head had bought out Richard Sears's stock in Sears, Roebuck, which represented about one-third of the company, and was offering it at $90 a share. "Mr. Stotesbury was one of the people I offered this stock to, and he turned it down," Walter related. Some months or a year later, the stock had doubled in value. "Fresh kid that I was, I said,

'Mr. Stotesbury, you should have bought that stock from me. You'd have doubled your money.' Stotesbury responded, 'My dear young man, I can't make money in everything.'" Henry chuckled when he heard this and drew on his cigar. "But we can always try, my boy," he said to Walter. "Just keep in mind . . . Money is always in fashion."[8]

During the years when Henry was developing Goldman Sachs's underwriting business, Samuel Sachs had not remained idle. He traveled to Europe frequently, strengthening ties with the banking community that provided much of the capital to fund the new issues. As the firm's fortunes ascended and all the things that the old-line houses had pooh-poohed became the hot issues everyone wanted to get in on, the personal animosities between the two brothers-in-law continued to grow. Henry clearly resented Sam's social cultivation of their European contacts, especially the Kleinworts, and Sam was openly miffed that Henry, with his agile, imaginative knack for identifying new opportunities, was universally identified as the most important partner, the guiding light who was leading Goldman Sachs to the forefront of the financial herd. The two were unable to communicate without ending their meetings in storm clouds of frustrated wrath.

Their wives, Babette and Louisa, kept their distance as well, Babette finding her sister-in-law haughty and patronizing while Louisa and her family mocked Babette for her apparent passion for spending money on her wardrobe and decorating her home. The antipathy even extended to the younger generation, who, with the exception of Walter, had different interests and socialized in different circles, rarely mixing with one another anymore.

CHAPTER FIVE

War in the Boardroom

The new issues co-led by Goldman Sachs—114 of them in 56 different corporations—kept spinning out like a river of gold. Who cared if the venerable investment houses considered the retail sector short on cachet and long on risk? The average man had money in his pockets and free time to sample the good life. With the advent of the automobile, shopping had taken an even higher-stakes turn. The climate for bringing out new offerings could not have been rosier.

Clever manufacturers recognized that product development and marketing were becoming almost indistinguishable. The Brown Shoe Corporation pioneered the use of entertainment as a marketing tool and turned itself into a national brand, mixing a generous dollop of show biz into their sales pitch. They employed a troupe of vaude-villians, collectively named them "Buster Brown" after a character in a popular cartoon strip, and sent them around the country to perform in vaudeville houses and on busy street corners, singing and dancing, telling jokes, playing tricks with a little dog "Tige"—and selling shoes. By 1913, the company's advertising savvy had turned it into the largest manufacturer of children's shoes in the world and marked another success for Goldman Sachs's list of publicly owned retail giants.

Henry did not have to stray far from his home turf to recognize the gold mine represented by another of the firm's new clients, the Cluett Peabody Company. The company's business was started in the middle of the nineteenth century, when American men rebelled against wearing the formal Victorian clothing that had been considered correct for over a hundred years: long frock coats, silk top hats, high button shoes, and tall starched collars. The founders of Cluett, Peabody started producing collars on a commercial basis in a one-room workshop in Troy, New York, in 1851 and picked the catchy name "Arrow" to distinguish their product from other emerging brands. Their success was instant and no matter where you turned in 1913, you would run into "the Arrow Collar Man." He was the brand-new image—or new brand image—of the largest collar, cuff, and shirt factory in the world, and he soon became the symbol of good taste in the men's fashion field. Women developed crushes on him, writing over a thousand fan letters a week that even included a marriage proposal or two. His good looks and the sophisticated lifestyle he led in the world of print propelled the sales of Arrow collars and shirts to $32 million by 1918.

One would imagine that in an era of innovation and prosperity such as blanketed America in 1914 the world would settle into a period of harmony and calm, but that was not to be the case. One declaration of war followed another across Europe in the wake of the June 28, 1914, assassination of Archduke Franz Ferdinand, heir to the throne of Austria-Hungary.

While President Woodrow Wilson preached noninvolvement, telling Americans to remain "neutral in fact as well as in name" and "impartial in thought as well as in action," dinner conversations from coast to coast became partisan and animated, with most Americans strongly supportive of the Allies. Many cited the latest news from Berlin, which reported the capital was "afire with war fever." Crowds there had mobilized in front of the French embassy cheering for war, and German factories had geared up for mass production of planes, warships, munitions, and field artillery. But there were those Americans who thought all the activity was strictly a matter of self-defense and held opposing sympathies. Henry was notably among them.

The atmosphere of conflict between Henry Goldman and his brother-in-law Sam Sachs moved in lockstep with the violence erupting abroad. It seemed, in fact, to worsen as their political sympathies moved farther and farther apart. Sam, a rock-ribbed Republican, felt the British and the French were utterly blameless and could do no wrong. He had been appalled when Henry switched his allegiance to Woodrow Wilson and the Democratic Party two years earlier while the monetary reforms of the Federal Reserve Act were coalescing. Now it was simply beyond him why Henry was so vociferous in his support of the German cause.

Their festering animosity came to a head with the foreign exchange squeeze in which Goldman Sachs was caught in the spring of 1915. Amongst realtors, the mantra is "Location, location, location." In the world of finance, it's "Timing, timing, timing," which can lead an investor to triumph or to disaster with the speed of a Ferrari. Blocks of European currency that had been loaned against future purchases of securities on the New York Stock Exchange were coming due in a matter of weeks, and the firm and its clients had to cover large amounts of money when the contracts matured. Making things worse, the sterling exchange rate had jumped from $4.86 to $7.00 to the pound in a matter of days. As the maturity dates approached, the firm's clients were forced to buy pounds to meet their obligations in London. Only two refused, stating that paying off their debts would inflict sizable personal losses. Both welchers, Julius Forstmann of the woolen merchant family and Henry Schniewind of Susquehanna Mills, were outspokenly pro-German, which exacerbated Sam's sharp-edged criticism of Henry's point of view.[1] He pleaded with Henry to stop applauding Germany in public and to refrain from pillorying the British for blockading German shipping lanes. His exhortations fell on deaf ears. He reminded Henry that the default of the two German sympathizers had cost Goldman Sachs dearly—the firm had had no choice but to cover their losses in order to retain the confidence of the financial community. Henry responded that future trading on behalf of the two delinquents' accounts would undoubtedly absorb all the losses.

The tension between the two was palpable, and it began to rub off on the families' personal relationships with one another. Paul Sachs, unable to stomach the unsettling fireworks any longer, withdrew his shares and hastened his departure for Wellesley College, where he had been offered a professorship in fine arts. His brother Arthur, fully supportive of his father, dropped the middle initial "G." (presumably for Goldman) from his name and barely spoke to his uncle. The cheerful family get-togethers, at which cousins who had once been close had joshed and gossiped and laughed, became strained and standoffish. When Robert Goldman, recalled from the West, received his sheepskin from college, he received a leather-bound set of Shakespeare's works from Uncle Julius and Aunt Rosa—and a ten dollar bill from Uncle Sam and Aunt Louisa. Babette was outraged at the snub and the mean-spiritedness from which it sprang, but Henry shrugged it off, breathed a sigh of relief that his son had graduated, and made a $5,000 donation to the Williams College endowment fund.

There were many apart from Henry who spoke up for the Prussians. Among them was John T. Adams of Iowa, a prominent pacifist who was running for election as national chairman of the Republican Party. In a letter to the *New York Times* from Berlin, he asserted that there were "no more peace-loving people in the world than the Germans, and that there were no people who had progressed further in all that [was] best in culture and civilization. But Germany in recent years," he continued, "has surpassed all other countries in Europe in prosperity, and she has interfered with the foreign commerce of Great Britain." This, he purported, was why the British "hypocrites, the 'bloody shirt' politicians of France and the degenerate aristocracy of Russia" were working round the clock to assure the outbreak of hostilities.

Adams further accused these powers of using the Austrian determination to punish the Serbian assassins of their monarch as a pretext for France, with England's support, to march her troops through Belgian territory to flank the right wing of the German army. "When Germany crossed the Belgian border first, that was England's excuse for declaring war, but not her reason. She had already decided that this was the opportunity to restore her commercial supremacy by helping . . . to destroy the German Empire," he concluded, adding, "But they will not destroy [her]. The hostile preparations which have been going on in France and Russia for several years have been too evident and too threatening for Germany to ignore, so they have prepared themselves . . . and will defend their homes and their rights."

Even the most casual social exchanges couldn't avoid circling back to the inevitability of impending hostilities. Over coffee with Phil Lehman at the St. Regis Hotel, Henry asked his friend if he had seen Will Rogers in the new *Ziegfeld Follies*. The cowboy comedian had tickled Goldman's funny bone with his rope tricks and his tale of flying to France and visiting Nice. "They pronounce it Neece," the vaudevillian had said, as he performed a double loop. "The French don't have a word for 'nice.'" Phil loved the one-liner, but he was a poor audience for Henry's contention that the French were using Germany as a buffer against the Russians, and his insistence that the Germans did not covet a single inch of foreign soil. On the contrary, Henry applauded the Prussians for endowing their colonies with education and social progress in return for the raw stuffs and products they produced, a far cry from the autocratic colonial rule imposed by Britain and France and Belgium. Phil, like Sam, didn't see it that way and remained unconvinced.

All the while, Babette remained tactfully silent. She, too, had many German friends, especially in the musical world, and had been brought up steeped in German culture. Alma Mahler and Fritz Kreisler were among the shining lights who attended her popular

Thursday afternoon salons, along with the wives of Jewish titans of finance. She was more inclined to think of herself as a citizen of the world than an American patriot or a Prussian partisan, and she had no desire to get into a dispute with Henry, especially with their twenty-fifth wedding anniversary nearing.

She had planned a gala party for some hundred and fifty guests at their home and was trying to think up something unusual to highlight the evening's festivities. Just a week before the celebration, she and her sister Florence had attended the Carnegie Hall debut of a celebrated young German mezzo-soprano, Elena Gerhardt, whom the press referred to as the "Queen of the Lieder." Lieder are romantic, intimate songs based on German poems, generally accompanied by solo piano, and they are considered far more difficult to perform than opera. Gerhardt—very young, very handsome, very smartly dressed—had hundreds of them in her repertoire, but the most memorable were composed by Schubert, Richard Strauss, and Hugo Wolf, and all were sung in German. Babette was entranced by the performance and without hesitation determined to engage Gerhardt to sing for her guests, no matter what the cost. But the singer wasn't easy to persuade, having found the anti-German attitude of audiences in salons in American homes "rather rude and uncivilized."

Babette shrugged off the rejection as if she had not heard it. Over Elena's protestations, she exerted every ounce of her formidable charms and, speaking in flawless German, assured the diva that she need not worry about putting together a special program; everybody would understand German and she could perform whatever she liked best. Mme. Gerhardt was going to make her husband so happy!

The event was a sensation, and resulted in Elena Gerhardt becoming lifelong friends with both Henry and Babette, time and distance notwithstanding. Whenever she was in New York, the ladies would lunch and shop once or twice a week and the three would dine together privately and attend the Metropolitan Opera and the Philharmonic. And in the winter, they would always make a point of meeting in St. Moritz, where they took carriage rides through the deep snow and sipped hot chocolate with mounds of *Schlag* accompanied by tea sandwiches, dainty pastries, and caviar.

In July 1914 the German army invaded Belgium, swept through the Lowlands, and proceeded to cut a bloody swath toward Paris. The newspaper headlines were grim, replete with photos of French cities devastated by bombings, troops massing at the front, and stories of German atrocities, which were adamantly denied in Berlin. The French government fled to Bordeaux, followed by five thousand refugees, some in taxicabs with gas cans attached to their car trunks. Anyone wishing to enter or leave a besieged Paris had to have a military pass. Soon there were some 50,000 British troops joining the fray, and on the eastern front the Russian army joined the coalition to lock in their hold on the Slavs. President Wilson stood strongly behind United States neutrality, and protestors for peace paraded by the thousands down Fifth Avenue.

Babette was fearful for Henry's safety when he declared he would conduct "business as usual" and pay his annual visit to

Baden-Baden in the spring of 1915. There had been repeated reports of German U-boats torpedoing unarmed ships, but Henry was skeptical and insisted he would sail on the elegant British ship *Lusitania,* alone if necessary. At the last minute, she persuaded him to delay the trip. She had heard of a wonderful camp that was for sale in the Adirondack Mountains not far from the sprawling family compound where his brother Julius spent the summer, where they could share vacations with their children before they flew the nest. Wouldn't he at least agree to look it over? It was located on Upper Saranac Lake, whose unspoiled tranquility and beauty had become one of the best-kept secrets of affluent Eastern society families in search of a summer haven. But not everyone was welcomed with open arms. Certainly not if one was Jewish.

The blatant anti-Semitism of the place first surfaced in 1877, when the very "establishment" Grand Union Hotel in Saratoga refused to honor a reservation from the influential Joseph Seligman and his family. The snub kicked off a national brouhaha. Other resorts, notably the snooty Lake Placid Club, which would become the future host of the Winter Olympics, began running explicit advertisements whose headlines cautioned "Hebrews need not apply" and "Hebrews will knock vainly for admission." The term "Restricted" soon became part of the Adirondack vocabulary.

But when developer William Durant fell on hard times in the early 1890s and wanted to sell some of his properties, some Jewish millionaires including Otto Kahn showed interest, and the builder of the Adirondack railroad proved more impressed by cash than family trees. Over the next fifteen years, a minor land rush among both Jews and gentiles ensued, and the era of the Great Camps, as they were dubbed by the press, unfolded.

Henry's property, Bull Point, was situated on a prime forty-acre lakefront site. The first thing that greeted a visitor's eye was the boathouse, which served as an elegant "back door" to the property. It was connected to the rest of the camp, which encompassed a variety of separate buildings for sleeping and dining and entertaining, by covered walkways whose railings were made of unpeeled logs. Unlike the log-cabin Swiss chalets favored by the Lehmans and the Rockefellers and the Baches, who had also been attracted to the lake, architect William Coulter had designed an English Tudor country house, complete with gables, half-timbered walls, and brick chimneys, to which he added rustic log porches and lower-floor framing. Aside from the three-story main building, which contained the living and sleeping rooms, there were several luxurious guest houses sizable enough to accommodate branches of the family for extended stays and a hexagonal "casino" with a dining room, kitchen, and servants' quarters downstairs and a huge paneled playroom up above. Babette could visualize all kinds of decorating possibilities for the camp, and Henry indulged her, anticipating long walks in the woods and quiet times to let his mind roam, free of disruptive confrontations.

When they returned to New York, there was no question that it was just a matter of time until the United States would enter the war, regardless of the public's peace marches. American tourists and businessmen were fleeing Europe as fast as they could, along with thousands of Europeans. Samuel Sachs returned from Europe on the *Mauretania,* her bridge, funnels, and superstructures painted black to remain inconspicuous on the high seas. Among his fifteen hundred fellow passengers, one-fourth of them in steerage for lack of space in larger quarters, were the children of J. P. Morgan, Junius and Caroline, who were escorted to the New York pier by their father's immense yacht *Corsair.*

When Sam walked into the office on Monday morning, he called for all the partners to gather around the company dining table. Rubbing his hands together nervously, he detailed the gravity of the situation abroad. With all of Europe teetering on the brink of war, he could not imagine that any of his associates would fail to feel as vehemently pro-Ally as he did himself. While he was in England, he had assured Kleinwort Brothers that Goldman Sachs stood firmly behind Britain, and that all his partners concurred. To his disbelief and dismay, Henry had not only remained opposed to the French and British during his absence, but he also was stepping out from behind his normal screen of anonymity to defend Germany and had been conducting an active exchange business with German banks.

There followed a good deal of name-calling, with first one and then another of the partners stomping out of the room in furious frustration. Henry pointedly remarked that Teddy Roosevelt, the former president, and Henry Ford were great friends of the Kaiser. Roosevelt shared the Kaiser's vision of Germany's becoming a democratic monarchy, and Wilhelm had awarded Ford a Prussian Naval Cross for his economic support of the Fatherland. And how about the object of Sam's hero worship, J. P. Morgan, who was a frequent guest on the Kaiser's enormous yacht, the one that was currently cruising around Norway. Didn't his hand-holding counter Sam's hostility sufficiently?

Sam could not equate Henry's arguments with the horrors he had seen photographed in the French newspapers or the evil portents he had heard being discussed by refugees on board ship. Nor could he stomach the possibility of losing the firm's carefully nurtured relationship with its London colleagues. Throwing up his hands, launching into a Sachs temper tantrum of the first magnitude, he called his brother-in-law a militaristic Nietzschean, lacking either conscience or soul. The newly hired office boy, five-foot-four-inch Sidney Weinberg, was watching the action from the sidelines as he filled the partners' inkwells. Years later he commented that neither man could even consider he might be wrong.

When the president of the Anglo-French mission to the United States visited New York late in 1915 hoping to negotiate a $150 million loan for the war effort by setting up a public bond issue, he was turned down by his first choice of an underwriter, the German-Jewish powerhouse Kuhn, Loeb. Its founder and chairman, Jacob Schiff, would not participate without a guarantee that none of the proceeds would go to Russia because of its Jewish pogroms. The press jumped on the story, and headlines the next day blared that the firm had refused to aid the Allies.

According to Stephen Birmingham in *Our Crowd,* it was as though a funeral wreath had been hung on Kuhn, Loeb's door. Reaction in New York was shocked and silent; response in London was angry and loud. Overnight, the Kuhn, Loeb name became unmentionable anywhere in the world of finance. Doors on both sides of the Atlantic that had been open were suddenly closed. Derogatory jokes pillorying "the Wall Street Jews" were heard in all the revues and cabarets of the Great White Way, and fräuleins in Central Park were forbidden to let their tiny Christian charges play with children who might even look a bit Jewish.

The loan was subsequently placed with J. P. Morgan, and virtually all the leading Wall Street houses participated. The Sachs contingent was eager to counteract the public relations gaffe that had been generated by Schiff, which they felt reflected on the entire Jewish banking community, and they were gung ho for showing their wholehearted support for the war effort by contributing generously. But Henry turned the idea down flat, repeating that he intended to support Germany, not Britain and France.

A dilemma now presented itself, as the firm had two ironclad bylaws that had been mandated by Marcus Goldman from the outset. The first was to support its new issues with the partners' own money. The other was that Goldman Sachs could only make an investment if all the partners were in agreement. Heedless of entreaties from his partners and his sisters, who were embarrassed and urged him to cool down his rhetoric, Henry stuck to his guns and continued to speak out publicly about Germany's virtues and the rectitude of her actions. Samuel and his brother Harry, angry at being rebuffed and also perhaps a bit sanctimonious, went directly to the house of Morgan and entered personal subscriptions of $100,000 each—not such an enormous sum, considering their wealth—and told whoever would listen that Henry's statements were purely personal and by no means representative of the beliefs and loyalties of the firm.

But the damage was done. Headlines castigated the firm. Repercussions were swift, with the firm's London partners, Kleinworts, cabling to say that the ill feeling generated by Henry's remarks was so great the firm had become persona non grata in England. Then the Bank of England forbade Kleinworts from participating in underwriting the giant Jewel Tea Company, the first time they were not involved in a Goldman-Lehman new issue, and enjoined them from granting credits to Goldman's clients. Not long afterward, Kleinworts' principals were called before the Ministry of Blockade, where they were shown a large number of intercepted cables showing that Goldman had been involved in an active exchange business with Germany, using their intermediaries in South America as a conduit. Kleinworts professed to be "frankly astonished" and withdrew from any further exchange business with their longtime friends until after the war.

New subjects for argument surfaced in the office with every dawning day. One of the major blowups occurred when the firm took a pass on the French Pathé Film Company, which had been negotiating to become its next major new issue. Pathé, suppliers of films in the nickelodeon days, were pioneers in the field of what we call movie production companies today. They had amalgamated studios from many countries in Europe and helped them to develop and distribute moving pictures internationally. Henry vetoed taking the company public, not because of his political sympathies, but because he felt that America's economy had become overheated as a result of the war and that it would reverse course in the short term. As a result, he feared an issue of Pathé stock would not be successful. Sam and Harry and Arthur did not agree, and angry words were exchanged. "Some of our neighbors do not seem to share [his] opinion," Arthur Sachs wrote a friend in early 1917. "Almost without exception, there has been no new business done which has not at one time or another been in this office. It is a great trial of patience to run, as Mr. Goldman expresses it, 'a turning down office.'"[2]

With time hanging heavy on his hands, little phobias of Sam's began to bubble to the surface. He became a cleanliness freak, washing his hands every half hour or so and demanding fresh towels every time he went to the washroom. Always a hearty eater, he couldn't keep his hand out of the candy box and put on ten pounds in six months. Convinced that Henry's comments were generating a public hate campaign, he became paranoid about keeping the firm's funds safe. At one time he excused himself from a lunch meeting with Henry and Phil Lehman at Delmonico's to make sure that the office safe was locked. Phil joked that all the likely suspects were sitting right there.[3]

As the United States began to enter the war effort in support of the British and the French, a wave of patriotism inundated the country. Everywhere you looked there were massive drives to sell Liberty Bonds. Henry Ford, an avowed pacifist, changed his mind and became an enthusiastic booster, subscribing $5 million out of his own pocket and an additional $5 million from the Ford Motor Company. Celebrities sold bonds in theaters, department stores, and recreational centers in every corner of the country. Douglas Fairbanks, the heart-throb of the day, appeared at Lord & Taylor's department store in New York, and Theda Bara, whose hit show *Cleopatra, the Serpent of the Nile* was turning hundreds away on Broadway, worked the crowds in Times Square. Chicago, Des Moines, Hartford, Cleveland, Syracuse, as well as Manhattan, all surpassed their quotas.

But not even impending war could tame Henry's wanderlust. He had been virtually a transatlantic commuter for years, sailing with his family to Europe for summer vacations as well as attending to business affairs in London, Paris, Amsterdam, and Berlin. Travel was an intrinsic part of his makeup. Early in the new year, the Goldmans' friend Elena Gerhardt was passing through New York en route to a series of concerts for which she was booked in California. Since their paths last crossed, Elena had concertized all over Europe and performed for British royalty and the doomed Czar Nicholas of Russia. While she was touring, she and Babette had kept in touch with a stream of gossipy correspondence, critiquing and often caricaturing personalities, performances, and the passing parade.

Henry, who had never been west of the Mississippi River in the United States, could think of no more delightful way to pass the next two months than accompanying the diva on her cross-country journey. Keeping it a secret from the ladies, he arranged to charter a private railroad car that could be attached to express trains and would give them the opportunity to disembark on sidings wherever they wished, for however long might suit their fancy. The car he selected, the *Chicago,* was very luxurious; it had five compartments (four with large single beds and one with two beds), two bathrooms, a dining room with a kitchen and pantry, and a sitting room with a little balcony in the rear. The accommodations were lavishly paneled and decorated, and a tiny upright piano that the Polish pianist Paderewski, who enjoyed star status, had used on his travels was rented, so that Elena could practice to her heart's content while they explored the countryside.

According to Mme Gerhardt's biography, *Recital,* the three of them were joined by a young captain named Reid and two personal maids, a most efficient butler, and an affable black chef named Sam. The days were carefree, each one filled with memorable sights, and every night was a special occasion, frequently finished off with a few hands of poker, which were most often won by Gerhardt. There are snapshots in a family album of the group visiting the Chicago stockyards, picnicking at the cave dwellings near Santa Fe, marveling at the Grand Canyon, spotting buffalo grazing in Golden Gate Park.

And "we had the most delicious food," Gerhardt recounted. "Whatever we wished for the butler would order ahead by telephone, and it appeared on the table at the next meal. We made quite a game of it, and thought out the most fantastic menus, but the butler was never perturbed, and whatever we thought of would appear, whether food or drink. We became so spoiled that we found everything in the big California hotels—the Del Monte, the Coronado, Pasadena's Huntington Hotel—most disappointing and were always glad to get back to our coach and link up to a new engine to forge on."[4] Needless to say, there was always plenty of excellent chocolate on hand—an obsession in the family—as well as Benedictine,

Henry's ritual after-dinner drink, but never, ever any "food that wobbles," which Henry had always loathed.

On April 6, 1917, the day of their arrival in San Francisco, the Americans declared their entry into World War I. In spite of repeated warnings from the States, Germany had resumed all-out submarine attacks on every ship sailing into the European war zone, whether it was flying a neutral flag or not. Many American lives were lost, and world trade was totally disrupted. Additionally, communications between Germany and Mexico had been intercepted that proposed a German-funded alliance between the two, guaranteeing Mexico the return of her lost territories—New Mexico, Arizona, and Texas—in the event that the United States was defeated. In spite of a sinking feeling that tolerance would be lost and ruthless brutality would overrun the American way of life, President Wilson called on a joint session of Congress to declare war against Germany because "the world must be made safe for democracy."

The Goldmans' railroad idyll, which was to have looped back to the East Coast via the Canadian Rockies, came to an abrupt conclusion. As excited crowds gathered in the streets shouting "America at War With Germany!" and demanding retribution, the *Chicago* sped nonstop back to New York. There the three friends shared a sad farewell dinner at Luchow's, the famous German restaurant on Fourteenth Street, before Elena boarded one of the last steamers bound for Germany. The Goldmans would not see her again until 1921, when the war was over.

On June 5, 1917, all registered American males between the ages of twenty-one and thirty-one were called up for the first of three

drafts. Harry Sachs's son Howard enlisted prior to being conscripted, and after a short period of training at Fort Dix, New Jersey, was shipped out on active duty with the 26th Division. Sam's son
Paul, so short that he was considered ineligible for military service,
took leave from his position as assistant curator at the Fogg Museum in Cambridge to join the Red Cross and was sent to France as
a paramedic. In a letter to his parents some months later, he plain-
tively inquired about "the conspiracy of silence" surrounding his
Uncle Henry and asked if his pro-German rhetoric had impacted the
firm's reputation.

One after another, off the family went, some intensely proud to
serve their country, some a little reluctant. Handsome Robert
pleaded flat feet to escape serving as an infantryman, but enlisted in
Naval Officer's Training School soon afterward. Henry's nineteen-
year-old niece, Sarah, his brother Julius's daughter, was a political ac-
tivist and a fiery supporter of Zionism and Chaim Weizmann's plan
to create a homeland for the Jews in Palestine. When she volunteered
to become a nurse with the British troops who were battling the
Turks for control of the Sinai Peninsula, her passport application
was held up for months because of her uncle's stance. But her per-
sistence was not to be denied, and she marched into Jerusalem at the
side of the victorious General Edmund Allenby. And on December
18, his twenty-first birthday, Junie forsook his studies at Williams
and was accepted as a junior officer in the navy. Even the little office
boy, Sidney Weinberg, who had become a devout disciple of Henry's,
volunteered with the Coast Guard—and by a quirk of fate, was assigned to serve on the beloved motor launch Junie had donated to

the war effort. And through it all, Henry remained opposed and very vocal.

The last straw came when Kleinworts cabled to express alarm at newspaper articles in the London press that put Henry's sentiments on public record. When they warned that Goldman Sachs was in danger of being blacklisted in the City, Henry realized at last that he was not just speaking for himself, but that he was placing the firm's future in jeopardy. On a balmy Friday afternoon in early October 1917, he told his partners, "It appears that I am out of step." And in a letter to Kleinworts dated three weeks later, written on Goldman Sachs stationery embossed with "Save and Serve—Buy Liberty Bonds!" he wrote:

"Since many months I have been revolving in my mind to withdraw from active business life. I am not in sympathy with many trends which are now shaping public opinion. Moreover, the world's war has deeply affected my viewpoint of life. My partners have been good enough to meet my views, and to make my withdrawal from the firm possible at as early a day as December 31st, at which time it will be effective. It goes without saying that I retire with the best of feeling towards the firm and all of its members with which I have been associated for thirty-five years and to which I have given all that is in me."[5]

He did not copy the letter to his partners, who confided to a coterie of eager reporters that "he will continue to retain a desk at the office and will give his services to the firm in an advisory capacity." Of course, he didn't. On the afternoon of New Year's Eve, he removed his papers from his desk, offered his partners his official resignation, and his regrets, and walked out, taking with him his share of Goldman Sachs.

"My God," nephew Walter must have said to himself as he headed to the "21" Club for a couple of his customary martinis that evening, "what have we got ourselves into?" As the Sachs who had always been closest to Henry, the partner who realized the great debt Goldman Sachs's success owed to Henry's dynamic personality and creative genius, the colleague Henry mentored and repeatedly reminded that "Money is always in fashion," he probably had the most realistic assessment of the consequences the firm would suffer and felt the greatest sense of personal loss. And if not the most intellectual, he appears to have been the most pragmatic member of his family. In his memoirs he recalled that Henry was "an extraordinary personality, the original genius in Goldman Sachs, [who made] the first great imaginative contribution to the growth of the firm."[6] With a quick look over his shoulder, he was quick to add, "Of course, my father [was the one who] had the dream of making this small commercial paper business an international banking business, and it was he who formed the relationships with . . . foreign banking houses and money centers. He was the great conservative banker who inspired confidence. People only had to look at him to see what a wonderful type of man he was. They were a great team."

Others in the family spoke less charitably, professing relief and disclosing their embarrassment at Henry's behavior. A fictitious report was circulated about his departure, which alleged that he had withdrawn from the world of finance and was living in "disillusioned, disappointed" retirement in Germany. It was repeated so often that even its originators began to believe it. At the same time, his erstwhile partners began to blot every trace of him from Goldman Sachs's historical records. It was reminiscent of H. G. Wells's novel *The Invisible Man,* with Henry's past accomplishments being displayed for the entire world to see while Henry himself was totally eclipsed. This hypothesis, of course, flew in the face of fact, as Henry moved bag and baggage to the Fifth Avenue brokerage offices of Arthur Lipper, where he remained a special partner for many years.

Deepening the rift, Louisa and her sisters-in-law, always jealous of Babette's éclat and popularity, began circulating rumors about an alleged affair Babette was conducting with Sam's younger brother Barney, a prominent Mount Sinai Hospital neurologist who had trained with Sigmund Freud in Vienna. A man of charm and intelligence with a wry sense of humor and a quick tongue, he was often called as an expert psychological witness in court proceedings and had absolutely no interest in his brothers' fortunes on Wall Street. He cherished the Old World culture he had encountered in his student days abroad and was fond of mingling with people from various social and economic strata. Babette undoubtedly found him a refreshing change from the brilliant workaholic Henry who, for the past twenty-seven years, had been so completely wound up in business affairs that he rarely conducted a conversation about anything else. The thrill of an illicit romance could well have appealed to the pretty, flirtatious, much younger wife. But whether or not there was a sexual relationship is strictly a guessing game. Both Barney and Babette denied it. Realistically, one assumes there was scant opportunity for the relationship to blossom into anything beyond a warm friendship.

Besides, Babette was kept too busy twenty-four hours a day being Mrs. Henry Goldman.

At the same time, it was whispered by guests at Babette's Thursday afternoon salons that Paul Sachs's brilliant Polish wife, Meta Pollak, was involved in a long-term relationship with "a man well regarded in the art world."[7] An entry in Walter's unpublished autobiography confirmed the rumor when he noted that his brother Arthur confiscated Meta's love letters after her death and sent them to her children along with those of her paramour, saying it was "best for the family."

Henry's exodus did little to endear him to the rest of his family. He and Samuel Sachs never spoke again. Neither did Henry and his sister Louisa, Sachs's wife. The generations that followed never even made one another's acquaintance until almost one hundred years had passed.

As for Henry, he never looked back or considered himself a fallen star. A man of catholic tastes and curiosity, he was convinced the time was ripe for the turning of a page and welcomed the opportunity to ruminate on his future options and broaden his cultural horizons. Since 1912, when he had become acquainted with the quintessential art dealer Joseph Duveen and had purchased the first of his magnificent paintings, Rembrandt's "St. Bartholomew," he had been laying the cornerstones of what would become recognized as one of the finest small collections of Renaissance and Flemish art in America. Now free to spend his time as he pleased, he was able to pursue additional acquisitions by scouting important auctions and galleries. Within a month he had purchased Franz Hals's "Portrait

Rembrandt's "St. Bartholomew," Henry's first major art acquisition

of an Officer," a celebrated seventeenth-century portrait of a cavalier that had sold at auction for $24.80 in 1841 but commanded $175,000 less than a century later.

Since the German troops first marched into Belgium, furious fighting had taken place throughout France. The loss of lives, ships, ammunition, and material, at Verdun, Loos, Ypres, and Jutland was staggering. From all accounts, the Germans, Austrians, and Ottoman Turks had the upper hand in the battle. British ports were blockaded by German U-boats, France suffered enormous losses, and the Communist revolution threatened total upheaval of the social system in Russia. But once Congress declared war, the draft swelled the armed forces, and the divisions of the American Expeditionary Force, led by General John J. Pershing, landed in France and routed the enemy in a bloody battle at Argonne.

The Germans found themselves on the defensive. With the arrival of fresh infantrymen, the tide had turned, and it appeared inevitable that the Allies would sooner or later emerge victorious, although at the devastating price of a thousand deaths a day. It took only two months until the wind had gone out of the sails of the once-proud Prussian ground troops. They were exhausted, overextended, and outnumbered. The Kaiserin sold her jewels, including a fabulous diamond necklace that had been a gift from J. P. Morgan, to raise money for arms and ballast for a government that was rapidly running out of funds, but the proceeds were far from sufficient. Faced with orders to return to sea, sailors of the German fleet mutinied in the port of Kiel, and within a few days the entire city was under their control. The revolution quickly spread across the country.

On November 9, 1918, under pressure from President Paul von Hindenburg, the Kaiser abdicated and slipped across the border into self-imposed exile in the Netherlands, where he insisted that the Jews and Communists had been responsible for the Germans' defeat. Medical observers were summoned and pronounced him paranoid.[8]

Peace feelers were extended to the Allies, and just two days later, at 5:00 A.M. on the morning of November 11, 1918, an armistice was signed in the dining car of the private train of Supreme Allied Commander Ferdinand Foch,[9] which was parked in a forest near the front lines. According to renowned author Stefan Zweig's memoir, *The World of Yesterday,* the streets in every city of Europe resounded with cheers, champagne corks popped, and hostile soldiers embraced and kissed one another. All of Europe was filled with euphoric optimism for the future. The Stars and Stripes were flying wherever one looked as the war to end all wars came to an end. Eight and a half million troops had been killed and 21 million had been wounded. A conservative estimate placed the civilian losses at 30 million but it was undoubtedly higher.

The German government moved to Weimar and, espousing the democratic tenets of majority rule, adopted a new constitution. Friedrich Ebert was named its first president. Henry Goldman doubted that Germany was ready to adopt such a populist concept and instead advocated a return to a monarchy. But his judgment was voiced from the wrong side of the Atlantic, and his advice dissolved into thin air as rapidly as the smoke from his cigar. The treaty was ruinous, and as hard times enveloped the nation after the war, the German people searched for a solution to their plight and became enmeshed in the macabre web of National Socialism and, eventually, the extremist exhortations of a new chancellor, Adolf Hitler.

CHAPTER SIX

Phoenix Rising

The peace conference was held on the outskirts of Paris. As the German delegates, 180 strong, all military appointees led by Count von Brockdorff-Rantzau, traveled to Versailles from Berlin to receive the treaty terms, their train was slowed down so that they could not avoid seeing firsthand the devastation that four years of war had wrought. Homes, churches, and entire villages had been burned to the ground. Market gardens and vineyards were punctuated with bomb craters, and towns with pedigrees hundreds of years old had been turned to rubble and dust. When the delegation arrived, they were bused under heavy guard to the hotel, their luggage dumped unceremoniously in the front courtyard. For a week they waited to receive the Allied peace terms and to draw up their counteroffers, which they were never allowed to present. They were allowed to go out in the town to shop or stroll in the beautiful countryside, now abloom with spring flowers and budding trees. They could write and rewrite their proposals. But all was silence from the Trianon Palace, and so it remained for six long months.[1]

In New York, in the weeks before the peace conference began, Henry Goldman suppressed his innermost thoughts and took a wait-and-see attitude toward the meeting at Versailles of "the Big Four"—Britain, France, Italy, and the United States—who were entrusted with drawing up the terms of the peace treaty. He was convinced that the Europeans' principal goal was the preservation of their old empires and was deeply concerned by the conflicting priorities they expressed. Georges Clemenceau, the prime minister of France, advocated a treaty that would guard the security of his homeland and punish Germany so severely for the suffering she had impressed on the French that she could never wage war again. Great Britain also sought revenge, but the pragmatic British prime minister David Lloyd George worried about the economic consequences that might accrue if Germany were treated too harshly. The Italians, who had originally sided with the Germans but joined the Allies in 1915 after being promised the port of Trieste and parts of Austria and Hungary when victory was attained, walked out of the planning sessions in a huff and refused to commit to anything after Estonia, Latvia, and Lithuania were declared independent states.

The political wrangling in Paris was intense and frequently verged on violence. Henry was disturbed by rumors attributed to a wealthy American manufacturer, Louis Freedman, purporting to show that Wilson's support of the Allies had just been a result of being blackmailed by Chaim Weizmann and the so-called American Zionist brain trust, which included Bernard Baruch and Louis Brandeis. He heard through the grapevine that they had promised Britain to furnish American troops in return for creating a "homeland" for European Jews in Palestine after the Ottoman Turk Empire was defeated. This was not a surprise to Henry, who knew Baruch well and had never seen eye-to-eye with him on international affairs.

Wilson opposed the entire blueprint of the treaty developed by the European Allies and proposed a far less vituperative reconciliation plan. He enumerated Fourteen Points for peace, which included removal of all economic barriers, establishment of equality in trade conditions, and the adjustment of colonial claims in a manner that would satisfy the interests of the populations concerned, not just the victors in the war. The centerpiece of his program was the creation of a League of Nations to arbitrate disputes and prevent "the crime of war." If the Allied powers failed to implement the League, he said, he was absolutely sure that another world conflict would occur within the next twenty years.[2] Clemenceau and Lloyd George reacted with barely concealed contempt to what they considered Wilson's superior attitude and "new world" naïveté and pointedly excluded him from secret discussions they were holding to rearrange the map of the Middle East and the belly of Europe.

From the beginning of the war, Wall Street had languished, and activity came pretty much to a standstill. There was virtually no trading nor were there new issues; people in America focused all their interest on the news from abroad. Lacking a dynamic leader capable of helping the firm to bounce back, Goldman Sachs fell on particularly lean times from which it did not emerge for years. This, of course, did little to endear Henry further to his partners and the rest of his family.

Meanwhile, for almost six months the German people clung to the assumption that the peace terms would be based on Wilson's Fourteen Points. They convinced themselves that the Americans would persuade the rest of the Allies that their interests, economic and political, lay with a reconstructed Germany that would also be their partner in defeating the Bolshevist threat looming to their east.

With unbridled optimism, they minimized the consequences of their defeat and flung themselves into what German historian Ernst Troeltsch referred to as "the dreamland of the armistice period."

In Germany, theaters, dance halls, and gambling dens were crowded, as if the war had never happened. On Saturday afternoons ladies put on their prewar finery, shiny seams and all, and joined the top hats and touts at the crowded racetracks. Young people, cynical and disillusioned by the outcome of the war, revolted from authority and tradition and sought thrills wherever they could find them. Cocaine, morphine, and alcohol were the cookies and candies of the day. Hundreds of men in women's clothing and women with bobbed hair and thigh-high skirts gathered at gay balls. Atonal music and Cuban rhythms replaced Schubert, Brahms, and Schumann in the concert halls; Renaissance art could be picked up for a fraction of its worth, and cubism and nonobjective art became the rage. It was a bit like Nero fiddling while Rome burned, or Scarlett O'Hara watching Atlanta being devoured by flames.

Henry remained hopeful that France and Britain would be persuaded to go along with Wilson's plan, which he viewed as level-headed and fair. He, too, thought that "unless justice be done to others, it will not be done to us," and heartily agreed with Lloyd George that the German recovery should take place quickly so trade could begin again. But the French seemed adamant in their desire to ruin Germany economically and militarily, and the isolationist American Congress appeared to side with them. Bernard Baruch, the economic advisor to the U.S. delegation, was also disposed to extracting huge reparations from Germany.

The German delegates were finally summoned to the historic Hall of Mirrors in the cold, gloomy Hotel des Reservoirs in May 1919. The hall was packed with two thousand Allied witnesses. A table in the middle of the room was reserved for Hermann Müller, the Weimar Republic foreign minister, and Johannes Bell, minister of transport, who had been appointed to sign the document on Germany's behalf. No other Germans were allowed to be present, and German counterproposals of any sort were not given so much as a glance.

Clemenceau delivered the terms for the Allies. He spoke coldly and disdainfully and opened the proceedings by saying, "You asked us for peace. We are disposed to grant it to you. The hour has struck for the weighty settlement of our account."[3] The terms with which they were presented were met with dumbfounded amazement. Among the major concessions, Germany was to relinquish all her colonies, free Belgium and Alsace, separate herself permanently from Austria, turn the port of Danzig into an open city, reduce her armed forces to the size and authority of a city police force, demilitarize the Rhineland, submit to occupation of the industrial Ruhr, and transfer rights to the coal and minerals in the rich Saar valley to the French. She was to give up 15 percent of her territory, 12 percent of her population, and half of her iron and steel industry as well as her air force and all but six of her submarines. Reparations of £6,600 million were levied on her for the damages done in the war. But most resented of all, and vociferously denied, was Article 231, assigning total blame for the war to Germany and requiring Germany's representatives at the peace conference to confirm that in writing, although neither they nor most of their fellow citizens believed it was true. The German people felt totally betrayed. Their trust in Wilson and the Americans turned into the sort of deep-seated hatred that can only blossom among vanquished people who have lost their property and their pride.

At first the German delegates refused to sign, citing the saber rattling of the Triple Entente prior to the commencement of hostilities. All the great powers had falsely claimed to have mobilized defensively when, in fact, there had been huge French loans to Russia and Serbia to finance armaments and the Russians had overhauled their transportation system in order to speed troop movements to the German border. And the British, they said, while constantly whining about German aggressiveness, had not only marshaled an enormous fleet, they had lured the United States into entering the war by promising influential American Zionists a slice of Palestine at the conclusion of hostilities. The Allied commanders turned a deaf ear and threatened to continue the fighting, invade Germany, and extend the starvation blockade they had initiated unless there was total compliance within twenty-four hours. Although President Friedrich Ebert's chancellor and his cabinet resigned rather than be forced to ratify the terms, the German delegation had no choice but to accede. They were the first to sign the document and were followed, one by one, by twenty-one of the Allies' representatives. When it was all over, a crash of guns announced the official end of hostilities, and one could hear muffled cheering from the surrounding streets.

It was clear that the severity of the treaty's terms were unrealistic. "It is obvious that the architects of the Treaty of Versailles built a treaty which is falling down over their own heads," Henry told a *New York Times* reporter as he disembarked from the United American Line's *Deutschland* several weeks later, returning home from his first trip to Europe after the war.[4] Economically, Germany had been second only to the United States until 1917. Now, with the loss of incentive as well as material wealth, the German people were certain to become fatalistic and to have no more real interest in implementing what they were compelled to sign. "It foreshadows some great catastrophe, the nature of which no man can define," he told the press. "It is like Gotterdämmerung [the twilight of the Gods] for them."

It was only weeks until his ominous prediction came true. The huge reparations debt, which everyone realized Germany could not pay, and the need to rebuild Germany's industrial structure, combined with a strike by lumber workers in the Saar and the staunch French commitment to extract every pfennig by taking over the industrial Ruhr, resulted in a devastating budget imbalance. Germany slid into an economic morass from which there appeared to be no escape. Since the 1880s, gold had been the standard for all international currencies; a banknote from any country was equal to its worth in gold. Until the beginning of the war, Germany's central bank, which was privately owned, had had no problem backing the mark with its resources. But the war effort had virtually halved the country's gold reserve, causing inflationary pressure and an alarming decrease in the value of its currency.

A panicked government printed more and more paper money so that employers could pay their workers and factories could pay their suppliers. The result was runaway inflation. Laborers whose pay rose astronomically found they didn't have enough hard currency to buy the barest necessities, and people's savings accounts dwindled to nothing. Within two years the mark was a scrap of paper having no value, overprinted almost hourly with more zeroes.[5] Meanwhile, profiteers like the notorious industrialist Hugo Stinnes mopped up steel mills, coal mines, railroads, electrical factories, hotels, banks, and every commodity they could lay their hands on, paying a fraction of their worth with foreign currency.

The end of the war had created a totally different socioeconomic climate in America. The year 1921 ushered in the era of what became known as the Roaring Twenties or The Jazz Age, when the public paid little heed to what was going on politically and grabbed for the brass ring of self-gratification. Peace fostered a prosperity fueled by new, life-changing technologies, among them radio, air transport, and plastics. Everyone seemed to have money to burn and wanted to get in on a hot stock market where millionaires were made overnight. Investors were led to believe that their life savings were extremely safe. In only a few years, the Dow Jones Industrial Average rocketed from 60 to 400, largely due to margin purchases that gave investors greater leverage. Henry was shocked at the naïveté of those who had not done their homework on the fundamentals of companies in which they socked their savings and foresaw impending disaster.

The scene that confronted Henry and Babette when they checked into the Hotel Adlon in Berlin in the spring of 1920 was almost unbelievable. Once proud, untouched by bombing, the refined, elegant city they had known had faded like an old tintype. Pictures in the newspapers showed men pushing wheelbarrows full of worthless currency to the bakery to buy a loaf of bread or to the butcher for a pound of dubious chopped meat. There were shortages of coal, firewood, warm clothes, and shoes. The price of a cake of soap, a box of matches, or a bottle of beer might double, quadruple, or rise a hundredfold between noon and dinnertime. Many people were reduced to wearing castoff military uniforms and clothing made of paper, and wounded veterans were seen begging on every street corner. The shelves of merchants whose shops had been stacked with luxury items when Henry had come over to investigate the art market just a few months earlier were bare.

Amid the turmoil, the Allied Commission on Reparations summoned a German delegation to The Hague to designate the chemicals and raw materials that were to be delivered to the victors. The German representatives included Hjalmar Schacht, a naturalized Dane who had risen from a minor position at the Finance Ministry to the office of currency commissioner. Schacht, tall, forbidding looking, always formally dressed and wearing rimless glasses, was a consummate politician as well as a seasoned banking strategist. He was faced with the challenge of ponying up the nation's debts from empty pockets. He bluntly told the commission that Germany could not accept the terms of the Versailles Treaty because they did not have the economic means to do so.[6]

His first official act was to call a halt to the printing of worthless money and to introduce a new interim currency, the rentenmark, valued at 4.2 to the dollar, backed by a mortgage on all of Germany's industrial and residential land holdings. However, he needed to assure the rentenmark's value by underwriting it with gold. Aware that a workable solution would have to be presented to the Charles Dawes Committee of Allied financial experts, which was scheduled to convene in the near future to review the means by which Germany's economy could produce payment for her debts, he begged for help from the Bank of England. Together with Montagu Norman, governor of the bank, with whom he met in London as Big Ben was tolling the arrival of 1924, a plan for a Gold Discount Bank jointly owned by Britain and Germany was devised. Under the plan, the bank would extend a loan of sterling pounds to the German export industry for three years at a favorable rate for the express purpose of underwriting manufacturing that could be used to pay off reparations.

This arrangement, however, did not sit well with the Americans, who held the largest part of the debt. The Dawes Committee proceeded to lay down a revised set of rules stabilizing the liquid capital of the Gold Discount Bank at 400 million gold marks, half raised in Germany, half abroad, which would make the debt payment both equitable and enforceable. Fifty percent of the new bank's board of directors were to be Germans, the balance foreigners—not quite the same as the original plan, which had proposed that the German government and its all-German board of directors would retain complete control. Credit would be extended to German manufacturers solely for the import of raw materials, which would then be reexported as finished products, with the addition of hefty taxes and assessments for transportation. A large part of the net proceeds were to be funneled into the payment of reparations.

Schacht, by now elevated to the powerful position of chairman of the Reichsbank, had no choice but to agree to the new plan. He observed that "[our] only remedy is to attract foreign capital into German industry and mortgages and other long-term investments.[7] Once in operation, the Dawes Plan will assure that Germany resumes her old place as a constructive force in the economic affairs of the world." He noted, however, that although the Dawes Plan presented Germany with her best opportunity to establish some form of economic stability, it was the harbinger of an unrealistic, self-perpetuating cycle in which the United States would originate loans to Germany, which she would use to pay reparations to other European countries that would then use that same money to pay off debts to America.

Henry, who first met Schacht in March 1923 at a private meeting of fourteen international financiers held in an exclusive Paris hotel, thought he was a shrewd and capable fellow—but "watch your step with him," he told his son Junie, who had recently finished a year of apprenticeship in a major Paris bank. "He could be somewhat of an 'artful Dodger.'" Among those seated at the handsome fruitwood conference table were Premier Raymond Poincaré of France; Hans Luther, the newly appointed German minister of finance; and Foreign Minister Gustave Stresemann. The agenda dealt with alleviating the burden of Germany's reparations payments and discussing how best to redevelop the nation into an emerging market with the promise of high returns.

Henry was one of the first to speak. He certainly agreed that Germany's economic recovery was in the best interest of the United

States, which provided the country with most of its food and raw materials as well as being one of the largest export markets for its manufactured goods. However, he found fault with the Dawes Plan, which created a German economy completely dependent on foreign markets that would encounter crippling trade barriers when foreign industry began to protect itself against German competition.[8] Instead, he backed Schacht's proposed program, which called for the active promotion of foreign investment in German industry and mortgages and construction.

With his limitless Wall Street connections, Henry was undoubtedly in the vanguard of American investors loaded with cash who capitalized on the opportunities that postwar Germany presented. The United States was entering its celebrated Jazz Age, and investors were eager to put their money in anything, anywhere, at the drop of a hat. Following the lead of Henry and a clutch of seasoned, successful moneymen, Wall Street set its sights on every German business, municipality, and state, happy to extend all the short-term loans it could generate. Although Schacht repeatedly warned that it was foolish to borrow foreign capital for theaters, stadiums, municipal parks, and unnecessary autobahns when every bit of hard currency was needed to pay reparations, even large industrial firms took direct American loans to boost the production of goods for domestic consumption rather than focusing on the manufacture of export items that would attract hard currency.

The foreign investments fostered a short but artificial prosperity. A wave of mergers that produced huge trusts and cartels took place: Daimler and Benz joined forces, and United Steelworks Company became the second largest steel manufacturer in the world, only out-stripped by U.S. Steel. Six large chemical corporations formed I. G. Farben, which turned out most of the dyes, pharmaceuticals, photographic film, nitrogen, and magnesium made in Germany. Department stores became bigger and grander, edging out mom-and-pop shopkeepers who would join the Nazi Party ten years later in overwhelming numbers and view the American manipulation of their economy, and especially the involvement of Jewish bankers, with resentment. One can hardly blame them, considering that the influential German-Jewish Warburg family held seats on eighty-seven corporate boards by the late 1920s, that they loaned $25 million to the Gold Discount Bank, and that they funneled money into rebuilding the German merchant marine. Henry didn't involve himself quite so far; he kept clear of politics, concentrating strictly on financial affairs, and never forgot that his first allegiance was to American interests.

His support and promotion of the German investment campaign was so successful that a year later he was sent an invitation to a private luncheon with President Hindenburg at the German White House. "It was one of the highlights of my life," Henry told the newspapers in a rare Stateside interview when he returned home. "We met for an hour and discussed all manner of subjects in a lively, informal way. I was especially impressed by the President's keen interest in the United States and what is going on in the world generally. I truly felt myself in the presence of a great personality."[9] At the conclusion of the meeting the president also bestowed honorary German citizenship on him, which he considered the highest of honors.

Shortly afterward, Henry left for a few weeks' holiday in St. Moritz, Switzerland, with Babette and their dear friend Elena Gerhardt. While there, he received a letter from his brother Julius in New York pleading with him to take it easy and to pay more attention to the condition of his eyesight. "It is a foregone conclusion that even the most obstreperous Swiss bank will come round to you," Julius wrote him, "but do take time for a well deserved rest." For the first time in ages, he did, taking sleigh rides, going to the spa for restorative baths, and enjoying the clean, invigorating mountain air and the caviar and chocolate shops that lined the main street of town, with his two "best girls" at his side. Yet the telephone was always close by, and he was often awake, wheeling and dealing and configuring new strategies before seven in the morning or long past midnight.

By 1924, business was booming and social life was swinging in Berlin once again, heedless of the pervasive poverty still clinging to the countryside. The city was where the action could be found, and it had become the center of the avant-garde. Max Reinhardt was staging his elaborate productions at the Tiergarten, and Bruno Walter was conducting politically fraught works by Wagner and Strauss and Mahler at the Städtische Opera. Oskar Kokaschka and Gustav Klimt were rising to importance in the art world, and everyone was reading Stefan Zweig and Thomas Mann. Kurt Weill was the people's favorite composer, his songs belted out by his wife, Lotte Lenya. Gangsters and pimps were enjoying a heyday, just as they would in Chicago a decade later, and the cabarets and music halls were filled with drug pushers, hustlers, drag queens, and ladies of the evening

Time out in St. Moritz with Babette and Elena Gerhardt, 1923

wiggling their hips and batting their kohl-lined eyes to the frenetic beat of jazz.

It is difficult to imagine that Hjalmar Schacht, so involved with planning the German economy's rise from the ashes, was also developing a reputation as a first-class womanizer. His semi-estranged, headstrong wife, Luise, who later became a strong supporter of the Nazi Party, had fled the Communist antigovernment riots with their two children in 1922 and settled in Switzerland. But when Hjalmar was elevated to the presidency of the Reichsbank, she returned to Berlin and greedily grasped at the mantle of a reigning corporate wife. The family moved into a vast apartment adjoining Schacht's office on the top floor of the bank's headquarters on the Jägerstrasse. Luise planned all their social affairs and coordinated the guest lists for elaborate dinner parties at which they hosted foreign dignitaries and bankers. The gatherings were liberally sprinkled with members of the beau monde with whom she had never before had contact— social climbing was a skill at which she excelled—and she quickly learned the latest twists in dress, food, and entertaining from ob- serving her new acquaintances. It was only natural that she should have met Babette Goldman, renowned for her style on both sides of the Atlantic, and probable that they would be attracted to each other on many levels.

Babette was the key to Luise's introduction to many of the sym- phonic artists with whom the Goldmans had become friendly over the years, and Luise was happy to go shopping with her or invite her to share the Schacht box at the opera or the theatre. They lunched together, visited all the popular new gallery openings and auctions, and took carriage rides through the park, while their hus- bands pursued new ways to stimulate foreign investment in Ger- many. They never talked politics—by the 1930s Luise was a confirmed member of the Nazi party while Babette retained a dis- tant, rather liberal neutrality but was more inclined to focus on the world of art and music. Luise's hospitality was reciprocated when she and her daughter came to New York several years later and the Goldmans arranged entree for them to view some of the city's major private art collections, including those of J. P. Morgan, the Lehmans, and Henry Frick.

In 1924, an elite "Banquet of Bankers" was held at the Hotel Kaiserhof, the first "palace hotel" in Berlin, celebrated in the 1932 movie *Grand Hotel,* a million-dollar property where the who's who of the country congregated for special occasions and where, in the heyday of the Nazi regime, Hitler kept an apartment. The gathering was a mixture of capitalism and socialism, politics, banking, and the intelligentsia, mostly on a Jewish basis, and the primary objective of the evening was to discuss the future of the German economy. After the customary champagne toasts, Hjalmar Schacht was the opening speaker. "The future of the German financial system is far from rosy," he began, "but at least we have the firm ground of our new German currency under our feet. The ship of state was wrecked, but the crew has managed to escape."[10]

Henry was seated next to Albert Einstein, who stood out from the white-tied guests around the table in his leather jacket, crooked four-in-hand, and sockless feet. As usual, his white hair and mustache were wild and uncombed, and his pipe rarely left his mouth. The two men enjoyed a mutual friendship with the conductor Erich Kleiber, and both were great lovers of classical music. Einstein was himself an accomplished violinist, and Henry and Babette were enthusiastic members of the audience and patrons both in Europe and New York. The following morning Henry told Babette that the professor, who had become a major celebrity all over the world upon the publication of his theory of relativity, seemed thoroughly unaffected, charming, and friendly, unimpressed by his standing as the darling of the media.

Henry, who spoke fluent German, had found Einstein a compatible dinner partner, conversant on many subjects but particularly fascinating when he described his recent visits to the University of Göttingen, where a number of bright and very young physicists were working with Max Born, the future Nobel Prize winner, developing the theories of quantum mechanics. Among Born's young graduate students was Robert Oppenheimer, the brilliant American who would become head of the atomic bomb program at Los Alamos, and who just happened to be a cousin of Junie's best friend, Willie Kraus, who had died in the devastating flu epidemic of 1918. When Henry asked "the professor" to explain as simply as possible what quantum physics was all about, Einstein described it as the study of the laws that apply to the behavior of phenomena on a very small scale, the scale of molecules and atoms. The subject was very controversial at the time, and the Born group had sought Einstein's blessings in order to gain backing from the grant-and-greed group who guarded the government till. But Einstein had remained unconvinced. "In Göttingen," he told Henry, "they believe in it. I don't."[11] Oppenheimer's reaction to the professor's attitude was succinct. "Einstein is completely cuckoo," he said.[12]

As the soup course was removed, Henry asked Einstein what he thought about the United States, which he had visited for the first time in 1921 with the Zionist leader Chaim Weizmann, seeking funds for the establishment of a Hebrew University in Jerusalem. Although he found it culturally immature and barren, Einstein responded that he loved America. And of course America had demonstrated that it loved him, too. After his ship arrived in New York, the professor recalled, they had headed with their motorcade through the streets to their hotel, and it seemed as if every car horn in town was stuck. The same phenomenon had occurred in Chicago, where the professor played the violin at a dinner party; in Hartford, Connecticut, where they held a big parade in his honor; in Washington, D.C., addressing the U.S. Senate in his halting English; in Cleveland, at Princeton, at Harvard; and all across the country. All these accolades had been delightfully flattering but frankly puzzling to Einstein, who had morphed almost overnight from a publicity-shy scientist afraid to meet the press to a crowd-pleasing superstar adept at fielding interviews with a well-timed raised eyebrow or a quotable one-liner. He wondered why science, which was hardly a subject that held great appeal for the masses, should create such brouhaha. He hoped it wasn't simply a diversion from the financial collapse that was threatening the country.

The Goldmans returned to New York shortly afterward to celebrate Christmas with their growing family. They had hardly seen Junie's firstborn, Peter, who was a handsome blond toddler almost a year old, and their son Robert's children by his second marriage, Louis and Bobsie, had grown so tall and plump since their visit to Bull Point Camp in the summer that they were almost unrecognizable.

Babette was one of the first to install a flocked white Christmas tree and to adorn it with blue lights, and presents were piled around it for all the family members as well as the household staff. It was always difficult to select a gift for Henry, a man who was known for his generosity and philanthropy at home and abroad, but a surprise awaited him in a neatly packaged rectangle sent from Berlin. In it was a rare portrait of Einstein by Hermann Struck, sent with warm wishes for the holidays by the professor and his wife, Elsa. Henry was touched, overwhelmed.

"Permit me on behalf of Mrs. Goldman and myself to thank you most profoundly for the beautiful etching of yourself which you were good enough to send me," he wrote in thanks. "You give to the world and to the time in which you live so much of yourself, and I have so little that is worthwhile to give, that I feel particularly indebted to you for thinking of me in this manner. We hope around Easter time to be in Berlin, and I would consider it a great privilege if you would afford us the opportunity of seeing you there."[13]

It was only the beginning of a relationship that overcame time and politics, philanthropy and social awareness, and that introduced Henry to the inner circle of scientific discoverers. Before his departure for Europe in the spring, he received a letter from the Göttingen physicist Max Born. According to Born's autobiography, *Max Born, My Life: Recollections of a Nobel Laureate,* Henry became a great help in assisting his research and that of his colleagues Walter Gerlach and Otto Stern by contributing money for their experiments at a time when scientific instruments were very difficult to come by.

At that time a wave of interest in Einstein and his theory of relativity was sweeping the world. He had predicted the deflection by the sun's mass of light coming from a distant star. After observations during a solar eclipse in 1919 and laborious measurements and tedious calculations, the conclusion was reached that Einstein was right, and this was published under sensational headlines in all the newspapers. There was an Einstein craze, everybody wanted to learn what it was all about. "I [gave] a series of three lectures in the biggest lecture hall of the university on Einstein's theory . . . and charged an entrance fee to support my Department," Born wrote. "It was a colossal success, the hall was crowded and a considerable sum collected which helped us for some months. But as inflation got worse, it evaporated quickly and new means had to be found."[14] Just then, Born happened to run into a friend of his wife's in the street in Berlin who told him he was going to America to marry an American girl. Born told him to look for a rich German-American who still took interest in the old country. "Tell him I need dollars to continue my work," Born told him. Some weeks later, Born received a postcard on which was written "Your man is Mr. Henry Goldman" and he gave me an address on Fifth Avenue. "Write him a nice letter," the friend said. "He's coming to Berlin and will be at the Adlon Hotel." So Born wrote and received "a very charming response and a check for some hundred dollars" for his department. Then he went to Berlin to thank him.

Goldman, Born learned, was the head of one of the biggest financial institutions in the States, and had always sided with Germany. He felt that the Germans had been wrongly charged by the Allies with bearing all the responsibility for starting World War I. He proceeded to give Born almost a thousand dollars more, which was a huge amount for that time in Germany, and also underwrote the research of many other scholars.

In the spring of 1924, Henry and Einstein visited Göttingen and stayed at the Borns' house. He was shocked by the stripped-down simplicity in which such elite intellectuals were living. A few weeks later, Hedi (Mrs. Born) received forty large packing cases, sent from America on Goldman's order, containing clothing and shoes for the poorer members of the university. Several helpers were needed to distribute the gifts.[15] After Goldman's check had come to the rescue of Born's experiments, the work went on successfully. The determination of magnetic moments of atoms and later of nuclei remained the main object of their research, and twenty-five years later resulted in the development of atomic fission by Werner Heisenberg in Germany and the Oppenheimer contingent in New Mexico.

Over the next five or six years there certainly must have been correspondence between Henry and the professor, but none of it has survived the passage of time. Following the 1929 crash, which did not affect his personal resources, Henry spent much of his time in Paris, where the bourse was riding high and people were enjoying a state of euphoric well-being. There was a surplus of 19 billion francs in the state treasury, industrial production was booming, the trade balance was extremely favorable, and the City of Light had usurped Berlin's eminence in the cultural firmament. Although his eyesight had failed almost completely, Henry went shopping for works of art while Babette made her rounds of the haute couture salons and became recognized as one of the best-dressed women in the world.

But his heart always returned to Germany, where he had maintained close business and personal relationships over the years, and where he could identify with the intellectual and artistic culture and the strong work ethic of the people. In 1931, when the German banking system, which was almost totally dependent on the United States, turned topsy-turvy, he rushed to meet with the minister of finance, hoping he could help the country avert complete collapse. He was instrumental in persuading business acquaintances to make large investments in a variety of plants and industries and joined thousands of American tourists in lavishing praise on the clean, orderly cities, the trains that ran on time, "the wonderful, cultured people" who loved children and flowers, who were so friendly and polite, so energetic and efficient. Considering Henry's reputation as a great judge of character, it seems incredible that he failed to recognize those same people's weaknesses, particularly the eagerness with which they embraced their newly elected chancellor Adolf Hitler. He had managed to reduce the jobless rate by 75 percent in his first three years in office and had restored the pride the Germans lost at Versailles, steering the economy into a model of modern progressivism. He was unquestionably the most popular leader in the history of the German people, who enthusiastically endorsed the unified, militaristic New Germany he offered them in place of an assortment of loosely federated states with differing priorities and rulers.[16]

Einstein, meanwhile, had continued to work on his unified field theory, with which he intended to provide the human race a more complete explanation of the universe. He also waxed more overtly political, delivering speech after speech in Berlin and at Oxford extolling radical pacifism, which caused governments on both sides of the Channel to question whether he was, in fact, a Communist. On his fiftieth birthday, in March 1929, it seemed as if the whole world wanted to help him celebrate.[17] Little girls sent him candy and cookies, crowned royalty sent him glowing accolades, and Henry, knowing how much he loved to sail, commissioned a beautiful twenty-three-foot yacht with mahogany decks and gleaming brass fittings as a gift to him. It mattered not one whit that Einstein couldn't swim. He loved to cast off on the lake near his home and drift about, sometimes in the company of one of his paramours but more often alone with his thoughts and his equations. These were among the happiest days of his life.

A few weeks later, Einstein and his wife, Elsa, took off for a second trip to the United States, where he had been invited to spend two months working as a research fellow at the California Institute of Technology. He was quite unprepared for the renewed wave of public adulation that greeted him upon his ship's arrival in New York. Apparently that did not faze him for long, as he disembarked to receive the keys to the city from Mayor Jimmy Walker; celebrated Hanukkah with fifteen thousand people in Madison Square Garden; lunched with the editorial board of the *New York Times;* toured Chinatown in an open car; attended a performance of *Carmen* at the Metropolitan Opera House and enjoyed a midnight supper of omelettes, fresh salads, and extravagant chocolate creations with the Goldmans at their apartment. Reporters followed him everywhere. He was emphatic in telling them that he would never return to Germany if the Nazi party gained control.[18]

Upon leaving New York, Einstein journeyed on to his new position in southern California. He took an immediate liking to the warm weather and palm trees and loved the informality and often zany flamboyance with which Hollywood laid out the welcome mat. He attended a private screening of the antiwar movie *All Quiet on the Western Front* at Universal Studios, had a front-row seat in the reviewing stand for a parade of scantily costumed sea nymphs on grandiose floral floats in Pasadena, sunbathed in the nude by a friend's pool in Palm Springs, and became friends with Charlie Chaplin, whom he admired immensely. His every move was recorded in the newsreels, to the amusement and amazement of his friends in Germany, who could not believe their eyes at his antics.[19] However, his relationship with Robert A. Millikan, the Cal Tech president, was not nearly as sunny.

According to Einstein biographer Walter Isaacson, the two could not have been more disparate in their views of either science or politics. Millikan was a Nobel Prize–winning physicist who was in the process of building Cal Tech into one of the world's premier scientific institutions, and it was quite a feather in his cap to have succeeded in bringing Einstein on board. He had been honored for verifying experimentally Einstein's photoelectric equation, and yet he was so conservative scientifically that he still balked at endorsing the professor's interpretations of many phenomena. On the political side, he was a rock-ribbed Midwestern conservative and supported patriotic militarism as vigorously as Einstein spoke out against it.[20] His board of directors and patrons were, like himself, very right wing and expressed alarm at Einstein's pacifist and socialist outpourings and tried to keep him from expressing in public opinions about anything other than science.

The professor's newly formed friendships with Chaplin and the progressive socialist author Upton Sinclair horrified Millikan, who tried unsuccessfully to persuade Einstein to drop them. How he reacted to Einstein's address to the Cal Tech student body at the end of the term, in which the professor questioned whether the harnessing of science had done more good than evil in our world, can only be imagined. "During war," Einstein had said, "[science] gave people the means to poison and mutilate one another, and in peacetime it . . . made our lives hurried and uncertain."[21] The chief objective of science should, instead, be to improve ordinary people's lives. Although a return to Pasadena had been contracted, Einstein's relationship with the administration there was on extremely shaky ground.

At the end of 1931, Einstein wrote in his diary that he was thinking of becoming a "bird of passage." He was finding the political scene in Germany more than a little disquieting, and despite mixed emotions about leaving his adopted home in Berlin, he was giving serious consideration to invitations he had received from universities in Holland and Belgium, France and Spain. He was no longer indecisive when he learned that his summer cottage had been raided by the Nazis, who supposedly were searching for a cache of Communist arms. While they were at it, they confiscated the boat he had received as a birthday gift from Henry Goldman, which had given him so much pleasure. Vowing he would never return, he boarded a ship bound for England. When it docked in Antwerp en route, he turned in his passport at the German consulate, renounced his German citizenship, and wrote a letter of resignation to the Prussian Academy with which he had been affiliated for nineteen years.

"Because of Hitler, I don't dare step on German soil," Einstein told a friend. "As long as I have any choice in the matter, I shall live only in a country where civil liberty, tolerance and equality of all citizens prevail. These conditions do not exist in Germany at the present time."[22] Just two months later, the German government passed a law stating that Jews could not hold official positions in government or the universities. Among those who were booted out and became refugees from fascism were fourteen Nobel laureates and twenty-six of the sixty theoretical physicists in the country.

For a while, the professor settled in at Oxford University, cushioned by the cozy assurance that Millikan wanted him to make his permanent home in Pasadena. But after the breezy informality and unfettered enthusiasm of the States, he found Oxford's hallowed halls self-satisfied and stultifying. It seemed like a gift from heaven when he was unexpectedly approached by the American educational reformer Abraham Flexner, who was in the process of establishing a haven for scholars in Princeton, New Jersey, with money donated by the Bamberger's Department Store heirs. It was to be called the Institute for Advanced Study and was adjacent to but not a part of the college, which had emerged from its snobbish, anti-Semitic roots to become a first-rate center for learning, particularly in the field of mathematics. Henry had been one of the Institute's benefactors from the beginning, and his niece, archaeologist Hetty Goldman, was slated to become one of its renowned academics.

The Institute was not founded as a teaching facility but as a haven for scholars, a center for thinking and research, and Flexner administered it with an iron hand. He was a member of the elite circle of foundation administrators who were often consulted in matters of philanthropy by the Carnegies, the Rockefellers, and the

Whitneys. He wooed Einstein well, offering "economic freedom" and the collaboration of other high-powered scientists and mathematicians, many also recent refugees from the Nazi regime, as well as the promise to retain Einstein's long-time assistant and mathematician, Walther Mayer. But he was also extremely controlling and kept a tight rein on all of Einstein's personal affairs, professing that he wanted to shield him from an overdose of publicity—which Einstein actually relished—and maintain his personal dignity as well as that of the Institute. He also warned Einstein continually that Jews like themselves should keep a low profile because too much exposure could arouse anti-Semitism, particularly in the waspish Princeton community.

When Einstein agreed to appear as a violinist at a charity concert in New York for the benefit of European Jewish refugees, an infuriated Flexner tried to upend the arrangement by telephoning the organizers and saying he would "fire" Einstein if he showed up. Press interviews, even with the Princeton student newspaper, were ruled out. He withheld all mail addressed to Einstein and declined invitations on his behalf, even one issued by the White House. "Your safety in America depends on your silence and the rejection of all public appearances," he told the professor.[23]

Under these circumstances, his freedom curtailed, kept out of touch with the outside world, the sizable speaking fees he commanded removed from his reach, it is not surprising that Einstein rebelled and became increasingly unhappy in his new surroundings. He referred to the Institute as "Concentration Camp, Princeton" in a letter to New York's Rabbi Stephen Wise, and wrote to his friend

Henry Goldman asking him to intervene with Flexner on his behalf. He knew Goldman had the interests of both the Institute and himself at heart and would be a fair and just intermediary in petitioning for changing the terms of his employment at Princeton.

Einstein was walking a slender tightrope when he presented his proposals to Henry. Although committed to defending his dignity and independence, he was timorous of burning all his bridges at the Institute, since he needed the money. A number of his relatives abroad relied upon him for support, and having broken his ties with Oxford and the University of Madrid, he hadn't a lot of other financial options to fall back on. Not wishing to cast aspersions on the Institute, whose lofty goals he respected and admired, he proposed that he would take a sizable cut in salary, which at the time was a modest $4,000 a year, and relocate to a small town in France where he could publish his papers from a little office and operate as a visiting professor at Princeton. He promised not to entertain offers from other American universities (Millikan was evidently still in hot pursuit) and said he would do everything within his power to keep word of the ongoing acrimony quiet, since hanging out the dirty laundry would just lead to more friction and heighten the growing tendency in America toward anti-Semitism.[24]

In a subsequent letter to Henry, dated just a few days later and most likely reflecting advice he received from Henry's brother Julius, the Goldman Sachs attorney, the professor sounded a little less contentious. He now volunteered to remain at the Institute under the original terms of his contract, provided that Flexner mind his own business. And he gave the Institute's "management" free rein to terminate his employment and retain him as an "external" member of the faculty if they continued to find fault with the way he handled his affairs and their relationship proved to be less than harmonious. But as a last resort, he felt that morally and legally he should be offered an equivalent opportunity to change the terms of their relationship.[25]

World events soon made Einstein's threats to quit the Institute, and Henry's intercessions on his behalf, irrelevant. The forces of change were swift and profound in Europe, and attitudes that had been festering for years bubbled to the surface. When Henry returned to Berlin in the spring of 1933, he found a very different city than he had left a year earlier. There were armed brownshirts wearing swastikas on their sleeves guarding the entrances to Jewish-owned department stores. It was difficult for him to get restaurant reservations or prime seats for the Philharmonic, and the friendly old waiters who had served them at the Romanische Café and the ice cream parlors on the Kurfürstendamm now seemed aloof and estranged. Friends and associates Henry had known for years crossed the street to avoid speaking to him, and in spite of the fact that he walked with the white cane of a blind man, he was frequently pushed and shoved about by passersby.

In April he wrote a letter to his brother Julius reversing the opinions he had voiced two years earlier.

If I were to attempt to give you a picture of only a small part of what I am seeing, studying and learning here I would be compelled to write you a volume instead of a letter, and for obvious reasons if this is to reach you I cannot say all I would like to tell you. While the American press informs you quite accurately, it nevertheless does not bring you anything like the real story so far as the Jews here are concerned. The press here is completely and hermetically muzzled and the government now in power controls every avenue of publicity to the effect that a system of intimidation and terror obtain.

I am probably one of a very few Hebrews now here who may be able to give the information that will be necessary in the relief action which Americans, Jews and Gentiles, may [need] to undertake. Thousands of intellectuals, teachers, professors, jurists, medical men, are being ruthlessly thrown out and being made breadless and tens of thousands of men of business are in the most Machiavellian way rendered unable to carry on. For instance, all drugstores received instructions not to sell medicines produced by a Jewish factory, to the effect that such concerns are practically put out of business overnight. All Jewish physicians are barred from the practice of routine examinations, which constitutes 60 to 80% of their practice. All teachers of Jewish origin unto the third generation are barred from activities and put into the street overnight without pensions. A refined system of cruelty has been meted out to the Jews. . . . the old will be partially permitted to carry on until by natural processes they die, but so that no after growth will be possible they will be enjoined from procreating. The same fate is meted out to Gentiles guilty of liberalism in any form whatsoever. I see many people in all walks of life and everywhere I encounter a spirit of taciturn depression.

But do not conclude that there is no opposition to this trend. Everybody whom I see, and there are many Gentiles among them, are fire and flame in opposition. There are millions here who are opposed to what is going on, but thus far there has been no possibility for such kindred spirits to meet. No newspaper can publish a protest, no hall can be had in which to hold a meeting because its owner would be certain of its demolition, and no meetings can be held in the open without certain bloodshed. I feel convinced that it cannot last very long and that the present is a bridge to the reestablishment of monarchy.[26]

Despite the growing list of attacks and prohibitions against the Jews, Henry clung to the faint hope that truth would emerge from behind the Nazis' smokescreen of propaganda, and the "good people" in Germany would condemn the brutality and restore sanity.

Soon after, some forty thousand "ordinary citizens" looted libraries and private homes, systematically stripping them of armloads of books. A gang of Hitler Youth students and beer-hall thugs carrying torches formed a bucket brigade to toss them into a huge bonfire in front of the Berlin opera house. The police, under the guidance of Chief Wolf von Helldorf, a virulent anti-Semite, took little notice and resolutely looked the other way.[27] The highest government sources professed ignorance as to who had organized the rioting, and much of the American press, marching to the tune of *The Christian Science Monitor* and the "radio priest" Charles Coughlin, dismissed the ruckus as "just a side show." It was difficult to believe that such a violent, vitriolic uprising was taking place in a country

where Jews had been fully integrated and which visitors from abroad
had lauded as a model of economic peace and prosperity, her citizens
well fed, well dressed, clean and happy and productive. Secretary of
State Cordell Hull was skeptical of the few unsanitized newspaper
reports, such as those posted by William Shirer of CBS and *The
Chicago Tribune's* Edmund Taylor, and branded them "exaggera-
tions" and "wild rumors." And former president Herbert Hoover,
unwilling to embroil the United States in yet another European al-
tercation, asked the public to avoid putting faith in "unsubstanti-
ated hearsay," although he retracted the statement five years later,
castigating the German government for its persecution of the Jews
but absolving the German people.

Not long after the book burning, the ocean liner *Bremen* sailed
into New York Harbor, the swastika flying boldly from her mast.
Among her distinguished passengers were the prominent British film
actor George Arliss and the Culbertsons, Ely and Josephine, who
had transformed the ancient game of whist into a game that was all
the rage, auction bridge. Henry wrote in a letter: "A fifteenth century
reign of terror exists there. I'll not return to Germany while present
conditions continue."[28] Little did he know he would not see his
beloved Germany ever again.

Contrary to what some may have assumed, in spite of his Jewish heritage, Henry Goldman was no Zionist. He was, in fact, far
more partisan to assimilating German Jews into the American
lifestyle and regarded Palestine as a sanctuary for persecuted Jews
and a seat of Jewish learning, not as a prospective sovereign Jewish
state. He revered scholarship and considered organized religion of

any kind irrelevant in his life. But he felt a strong moral duty to present President Franklin Delano Roosevelt with a firsthand report on the dangerous state of affairs facing the Jews in Germany and to plead for liberalization of the tight immigration guidelines adopted during the Hoover administration. He turned to an old friend, Henry Morgenthau Jr., who had recently been named secretary of the treasury, for an introduction.

Morgenthau was not encouraging. He and his attorney, Randolph Paul, had contacted Roosevelt just a few weeks earlier with a plan for a covert operation to buy exit visas for hundreds of Jewish families attempting to escape from Romania. The president had turned a deaf ear, saying he was reluctant to get involved in activities that might "create economic and financial disturbances" or draw the United States into "another European conflict." At a time when isolationism, appeasement, and pacifism were strongly endorsed in America, he was not about to wreck the domestic agenda of his initial term on the shores of foreign affairs. (As Paul's daughter-in-law recently commented, it was not Roosevelt's "shining hour.")

During the 1933 Christmas holidays, Albert and Elsa Einstein attended a festive dinner for a few special friends at the Goldmans' New York apartment. Among the glittering guests were the renowned Austrian violinist and composer Fritz Kreisler, maestro Arturo Toscanini with his wife and his daughter Wanda, and the author Thomas Mann. Everyone was talking about the spectacular Metropolitan Opera debut of the Norwegian Wagnerian soprano Kirsten Flagstad in *Die Walküre* and the astounding success of Pearl Buck's novel *The Good Earth,* which had been awarded the Pulitzer

Prize in 1932. Buck would go on to win the Nobel prize for fiction writing in 1938.

Einstein brought up the fact that he had recently been asked for an interview by members of President Roosevelt's staff who wanted to get the real lowdown on the plight of the Jews in Germany. A good deal of confusion about the situation appeared to exist due to the extensive propaganda campaign being waged in America by the German government. Einstein was hopeful that Henry would agree to be interviewed as well, since he had visited Berlin so recently, and also wondered whether Henry would allow him to tell reporters what Hans Luther, the former head of the Reichsbank, who had recently been named ambassador to the United States, had allegedly told him with respect to the German Jewish problem. As Einstein recalled it, Luther was quoted to have said, "Who cares if half a million Jews are killed?"[29]

Henry denied any knowledge of this exchange. "Dr. Luther never made this remark to me and I cannot imagine from what source you gathered this impression. . . . May I suggest that if any of us are interviewed by men in the entourage of the president, we must all be exceedingly careful not to become victims of gossip and of hearsay, because a wrong step might be fatal to the cause which is so near to our hearts."[30]

Two weeks later, Henry was invited to a private lunch with Roosevelt at the White House. The president was a cordial and gracious host, insisting on personally mixing martinis, for which he was famous, before they began to eat. Henry, who rarely drank anything stronger than a glass of wine with dinner or a pony of Benedictine before bed, sampled the drink abstemiously. He had important matters on his mind, and he was not one to waste time on small talk. But whenever he attempted to bring up the subject of the atrocities he had witnessed or the mobs of frantic Jews beating on the doors of American consular offices hoping to obtain visas, Roosevelt would sidestep adroitly and start chatting about the Yankees' batting record or the chances for the States to win the America's Cup races. As the two prepared to say their farewells, the president gestured with his cigarette holder and told Henry that the Germans were surely treating the Jews dreadfully, but it could not be a government affair, particularly for a newly elected administration, in a time of economic uncertainty.

The commander in chief may have chosen to be politically color blind—members of the fourth estate frequently observed that he was "always tremendously interested in public opinion" and "felt more secure when he thought the public was behind him"—but many movers and shakers in the private sector were not. They were shocked that the paltry number of German Jews allowed to immigrate was boosted to just five thousand a year, far less than half the number who had been accepted in 1906. Among those moved to action was Henry's brother Julius. A successful New York corporate lawyer, he was one of the founders of the Federation for the Support of Jewish Philanthropic Societies and the father of a noted radiologist, a leader in domestic oil exploration, and a famous woman archaeologist. He proceeded to enlist the support of hundreds of generous contributors of varying faiths, many of whom donated as little as ten dollars—or as much as several thousand—to help evacuate minorities of all faiths and persuasions from Europe. Henry himself pulled strings and depleted his bank account to spirit the physicists Max Born and Otto Stern out of Germany and resettle them in England. He obtained assignments at leading American campuses for Adolph Goldschmidt, the eminent medieval art historian from the University of Berlin, and assisted a bevy of scientists, musicians, doctors, and businessmen in obtaining papers, legal and ersatz, to leave Austria and Germany and establish new lives for themselves and their families in the States.

His wife, Babette, was no less involved. She was one of a small group of women who helped the United Jewish Appeal collect more than two million dollars in less than three months for the relief of Jews in Germany. While one hundred "trade chairmen" canvassed every business in New York, these six women volunteers approached wealthy financiers, entrepreneurs, and artistic luminaries on their home turf and using their social connections, their graphic descriptions of the mistreatment of minorities in Germany, and their charm managed to collect almost one-fourth of the drive's total proceeds. "Your grandmother was a real pistol," Galit Brichta, head of development for the UJA, said to me close to a hundred years later as she surveyed the list of those donors and the amounts they contributed. "Do you know how much that money represents today?"

Surprisingly, the humanitarian concern that inspired these efforts was not matched by much of academia. The influential Columbia University president Nicholas Murray Butler invited Nazi ambassador Hans Luther, whom he heralded as the representative of "the government of a friendly people," to speak on the campus and advised the students that he was "entitled to be received . . . with the

Babette in 1935

greatest courtesy and respect." Luther's speech focused on Hitler's peaceful intentions. Three years later, in 1936, Butler sent a delegate to Nazi Germany to participate in the 550th anniversary celebration of the University of Heidelberg, in spite of the fact that it had already been purged of Jewish faculty members and had instituted a Nazi curriculum and hosted a burning of books by Jewish authors.[31]

Dartmouth College introduced a quota system limiting the number of Jews it would admit. Harvard was no less lily white. In May 1934, the university's administration also played host to Ambassador Luther. He visited Harvard's Germanic Museum, which had been founded some thirty years earlier by Henry and six of his peers, and the Widener Library. The following month, Harvard president James Conant rolled out the red carpet for Hitler's foreign press chief when he attended his twenty-fifth class reunion. Ernst Hanfstaengl, class of 1909, had been close to Hitler since the early 1920s and was professionally responsible for spreading Nazi propaganda abroad. Surprisingly, even Harvard's student newspaper was supportive of the university administration's warm welcome and urged President Conant to award him an honorary degree. Another ceremony, hosted by the Boston consul-general in the university chapel, honored graduates from the area who had died while fighting in the German army in World War I. The consul's memorial wreath bore a huge swastika.

Even as the stories of Jewish persecution continued to mount and multiply, some American corporations chose to continue "business as usual" in Germany. The outspokenly anti-Semitic Ford Motor Company, which produced half of the domestic cars and most of the military ambulances in Germany, ignored the seizure of Jewish property rights and confiscation of the Jews' personal belongings. Even as "Jew-baiting" became official state policy, Standard Oil continued to pump gas in the twenty thousand filling stations it owned throughout the country, adding substantially to the nation's tax income. And a number of manufacturing interests snapped up lucrative contracts offered by Nazi concerns, heedless of the newly adopted Nuremberg Laws officially disenfranchising Jews and classifying them as noncitizens.

It must have been difficult for a didactic elder statesman of the financial world to whom so many had turned for counsel and advice for almost half a century to abandon his lifelong convictions and loyalties. But Henry harbored no regrets for his support of Germany before the World War, nor did he consider offering an olive branch to the Sachs dynasty in an attempt to patch up the differences between the two families. However, the events of the 1930s called into question the importance of the fortune he had amassed and the future relevance of the world of investment banking he had created.

Some three years later, at his second inauguration, President Roosevelt addressed a rapt crowd in Philadelphia. "To some generations much is given," he told them. "Of other generations much is expected. This generation of Americans has a rendezvous with destiny." Henry could only wonder: Had his personal rendezvous occurred twenty years earlier, or was there another act to come?

CHAPTER SEVEN

The Fine Art of Collecting Fine Art

As news of the violation and desecration of so much great art started to filter out of Germany with the tide of refugees, Henry became concerned about the disposition of his own beloved collection after he passed away. Although he was still an active investor for his own account, and very much involved in international banking affairs, art collecting had been his passion, his obsession, for over twenty years.

He had already started purchasing fine art when he was a student at Harvard. He had developed a taste for antiquity as a teenager on summer vacations in Bavaria and fell head over heels in love with the sculptures and carvings confronting him at every turn in Bamberg. It was like a living fairyland. Back home in New York, he spent hours on weekends visiting the Metropolitan Museum of Art, just blocks from his parents' home, and developed a sensitivity to art unusual in one so young. While he was a student at Harvard, unable to indulge in sports because of his poor eyesight, he scouted the Boston and New York art galleries and bought what attracted him aesthetically and was within his rather limited means. From the beginning, he told gallery owners he bought with his instinct and his eyes, not his ears. His first significant purchase was a sixteenth-century Riemenschneider woodcarving that cost him approximately $1,500. Among the eclectic acquisitions that followed were French Gothic wood carvings, sixteenth-century Flemish stained-glass panels, and a rare, huge Persian rug. For his entire life, he retained deep emotional involvement with each of his acquisitions, never viewing any of them as pure investment vehicles.

But it wasn't until thirty-five years after leaving Harvard, when he happened to meet the charismatic art dealer Joseph Duveen aboard the Cunard liner *Berengaria* sailing to London from New York, that he began considering collecting in earnest. By then Henry had built up a substantial fortune and a widely recognized reputation for his business acumen. Whether the meeting was by chance or chicanery is up for speculation. Duveen was known to orchestrate "bumping into" well-to-do Americans by wheedling information about their to's and fro's from trusted servants and chauffeurs and deck stewards. He was generous in showing his appreciation with hundred dollar tips, which ensured his continual knowledge of their every move, their every little desire, and ensured, too, that they remained under the scrutiny of Duveen's secret "spy system" until they said their last hurrahs.

Joe Duveen was a good-looking man, over six feet tall, with a ruddy complexion, dark hair, a bristling toothbrush mustache, and sparkling gray eyes. He had a marvelous infectious laugh, unflagging energy, and boundless enthusiasm for pulling off a deal. Babette said later that he reminded her of Gilbert and Sullivan's Mikado, with his over-the-top British accent and habit of clapping his hands to command attention, and she loved to mimic him. Variously called a manipulator, a smooth-talking rogue, and a charmer, no one could dispute the fact that he was the best salesman in the world. His influence on Henry was immediate. What had started as a sometime hobby became an addiction, and Henry ended up with one of the finest small collections of Renaissance art in the world.

Duveen's career was completely without precedent. In earlier times, collectors had bought directly from the artists or from the aristocrats who had commissioned their work. He created a niche for himself, playing the middleman, paying exalted prices for works of art in Europe and selling them in America at a huge profit. It has often been said that he rewrote the history of art with his checkbook. A self-taught authority, he liked to think of himself as an educator in the field of fine art, with the biggest names in industry and finance his eager and malleable pupils. He had inherited many of them, including Arabella Huntington, Joseph Widener, Benjamin Altman, and J. P. Morgan, from his British uncle Henry, who had been their interior decorator and who bought valuable antique china and furniture on their behalf. But Joe had bigger ideas. Just as Henry had steered Goldman Sachs into creative new endeavors, Joe had moved his family business away from its emphasis on decorative arts into something more speculative, more lucrative, and much more exciting: trading in Old Masters.

Duveen's "runners," the employees commissioned to follow the tracks of millionaires who were potential purchasers of exquisite and fabulously expensive fine art, undoubtedly had fingered Henry as a juicy addition to their chief's little black book as the stories of his wildly successful underwriting achievements and his interest in art proliferated. And so it was not too surprising that the two men were booked on the same transatlantic steamer that May of 1911 and occupied adjacent deck chairs. Over tea and cigars, they struck up an instant friendship that transcended their business relationship and lasted until the end of their lives.

They both were highly competitive men, viewing the hunt for new acquisitions as similar to a sport like golf or tennis, and had an almost visceral desire to surround themselves with the most beautiful things. It is said that Duveen would keep a newly acquired painting on an easel next to his bed when he retired so that it would inhabit his dreams. Henry, on the other hand, was so excited when his first major acquisition, Rembrandt's painting of St. Bartholomew, was hung in his living room that he tossed and turned and couldn't sleep all night.

Neither man tried to pretend that he was not a Jew, but both, by virtue of their brilliance in their chosen fields, were accepted in the highest social circles.[1] Although they were married by rabbis and buried in Jewish cemeteries, neither observed Jewish holidays or attended religious services. They were, in fact, entranced by Christmas and all its traditional trappings and spent hours refining their lengthy gift lists, making their friends and families and Cartier the jeweler very happy.

From the start, there wasn't anything Joe wouldn't do for the Goldmans. He arranged for private tenders to ferry them to shore in the midst of raging storms when they disembarked from ocean liners at Le Havre and Bremen. Baskets of orchids and long-stemmed roses in Sèvres vases greeted them at hotels around the world. Would they like a better cabin for the weeklong overseas voyage, or to dine with the ship's captain? Did they need assistance in getting opening night tickets at Covent Garden? They need only ask.

When the Goldmans' chauffeur left them to return to his native Germany, Duveen just happened to know of a gem who was available. His name was Eugene Scheck—big, gentle, and blond, and a skilled driver and mechanic. He became one of Henry's most valued and trusted confidants and remained with him until his death twenty-five years later. The children and grandchildren and even perfectionist Babette loved him unrestrainedly. Unless there were other passengers in the Pierce Arrow town car, Henry would lower the glass partition dividing the front and back seats so that he could discuss the ways of the world with him and get a bead on how "the other fellow" saw things. This was, of course, an arrangement that suited Duveen perfectly, as Scheck gave him clues to the extent of Henry's interest in a painting that was for sale or a sculpture he had seen or an insider's view of what was happening on the Street.

In the years just before World War I, Duveen was quick to recognize the growing desire among moneyed Americans to own Old Masters, and quicker still to convince them that owning great art would immortalize them. Of course, he assured them that he alone was the key to getting their hands on these rare and exceptional objects. It did not hurt his cause that many of the British and European nobility with great art collections were, at the time, in need of ready cash. And so he was able to cultivate and cater to a remarkable string of collectors, including John D. Rockefeller, Clarence Mackay, Jules Bache, the Lehmans—Philip and his son Robert—and the culturally undereducated director of U.S. Steel Henry Clay Frick, who was satisfied with pricey pretty things until he came under Duveen's nurturing wing.

Most of these collectors were purchasing in volume and battling to see who could outspend the other. Each wanted to create a
collection outstanding for its quantity as well as quality, which he
could flaunt as a symbol of success. Once they had entrusted Duveen to assist them, he was able to manipulate the market and push
prices to the stratosphere, pocketing his 10 percent commission and
becoming enormously wealthy in his own right. He arranged the
purchase of ninety-five of the paintings in the Mellon collection that
now hang in the National Gallery of Art in Washington, D.C., and
at least one hundred and fifty of Samuel H. Kress's seven hundred
works of art, most for upward of $200,000 and some for as much
as $1.5 million.

Henry's approach to collecting was vastly different. He was a
private man, modestly considering himself a minor collector of
major works, not seeking to impress the public like the Kuhn, Loeb
banker Otto Kahn, who had even retained the services of a famous
public relations consultant, Edward Bernays. His objective was to
surround himself with the most beautiful examples of art created by
man. Each painting or sculpture or illuminated manuscript had to
speak to him emotionally as well as intellectually. It was a very personal thing. Unsentimental as he was in his personal relationships,
he was deeply moved by great art and music and was known to weep
upon listening to a particularly beautiful rendition of a Brahms or
Beethoven composition on the violin or to feel light-headed when
he was in the presence of a masterpiece by Giorgione or Titian or
Rembrandt. What a chord this must have struck with Duveen, who
was known to exclaim enthusiastically about each new purchase.

In 1912, Henry and Babette took a long-term lease on the third floor of 998 Fifth Avenue, a brand-new building that the noted architect Stanford White had designed as a companion piece to the Metropolitan Museum of Art, which it faces. Geographically, it was only a mile away from the town house on Seventy-sixth Street where they had lived for the past fifteen years. But it was a giant step socially from the insular, primarily German-Jewish neighborhood on the Upper West Side, in which their children had grown up, to the more exclusive, more sophisticated—and far more expensive—enclave that was being developed on the opposite side of Central Park in what today is New York's most fashionable neighborhood. The apartment also was sufficiently spacious to serve as a backdrop for the new family Henry was planning to build, the one made of pigment and canvas and clay, and Babette's Thursday afternoon salons, to which the city's most prominent classical musicians, singers, and writers sought invitations.

The apartment was considered by the cognoscenti one of the most beautiful in the city, although due to the Goldman's penchant for privacy it was never professionally photographed. Babette, herself recognized as a tastemaker and an icon of style, engaged Elsie deWolfe, a former actress who was a protégée of Stanford White's and the most famous interior designer of the early 1900s, as her decorator.

Henry cherished each and every acquisition and knew their most minute details, even after his sight was gone. There is a story in the autobiography of the famous German physicist Max Born about a visit he paid to the Goldmans' apartment in 1926. Born says, "It was moving to see him amongst his pictures, which he described in every detail as if he could still see them. One day when Hedi [Mrs. Born] and I were with him, two experts from Harvard called on him to see his gallery, and he showed them around, with detailed explanations. When they were about to leave, he stumbled a little in passing through a doorway, and one of the men asked me, 'Does Mr. Goldman not see very well?' When I answered, 'He is completely blind,' the man looked at me as if I were mad. 'But he certainly sees his pictures,' he remarked. 'Well, he did,' said Born, 'but with the eyes of a loving memory.'"[2]

Unlike many of the collectors who preceded him, he did not begin by buying pictures of the Barbizon school, or English and French painters of the eighteenth and nineteenth centuries, and then develop a taste for the earlier masters. Henry's first major acquisition was a painting from Rembrandt's late period, when he was at the pinnacle of his achievement. It had been executed at a time when the acclaimed artist was overcome with great sorrow because he had been forced to sell his house and art collection at public auction and had lost his social position. It is a large portrait of "The Apostle Bartholomew," which was formerly a part of the collection of Princess Troubetzkoi in Leningrad, and has been called one of the most powerful representations of the types Rembrandt must have encountered in the poor Jewish quarter of Amsterdam near his house. The model was a poor man of the street whose expression reflected centuries of human suffering. Long after Henry's sight was gone, he still recalled how wrapped up he was in this picture and how his memories turned to it every hour with great love. But his joy

in the painting was not an end in itself. It was a stepping-stone, al-
beit a very important one, in a career of collecting that lasted more
than twenty years.

One of the outstanding paintings in the Goldman collection, and
ultimately one of the most controversial, was the dead Christ
mourned by his mother, known as "The Deposition" or "The En-
tombment," which had been unequivocally attributed by the acclaimed connoisseur Bernard Berenson to Fra Angelico, adding
considerably to its value. Berenson had, in fact, been instrumental in
obtaining the work two years earlier, in 1922. It was a Pietà in a
lovely landscape and had been offered to him by one of the middle-
men whom he had commissioned to search churches and palazzos
throughout the Tuscan countryside for hidden treasures.

Berenson's wife, Mary, raved about the painting's fine quality
and beautiful drawing and coloring. It had been created in the last
period of the artist's life and had never been cleaned or otherwise
restored. However, the wood on which it had been painted had split,
which would mandate transferring it to canvas should it be sent to
America. This was, incidentally, a fairly common practice in pre-
serving Old Masters and did not affect the painting's value.

Within a few months, Duveen had acquired the painting and, a
year later, had resold it to Henry, who repeatedly told everyone in the
art world how mad he was about it and hardly talked of anything
else. The icing on the cake was that Berenson had promised to write
a feature article about the painting in the distinguished publication
Art in America. It would be the definitive article on Italian paintings, and a classic.

Even so, Duveen cautioned Henry to write Berenson of the purchase and ask him to comment on its condition and authenticity before he made his final payment. "If you're going to spend a quarter of a million, you want to be sure it's the real thing," he said.[3] What Duveen failed to mention was that his firm had signed a very hush-hush contract with Berenson some ten years earlier. At that time, Berenson had been released from his curatorial tasks by the famed and very wealthy collector Isabella Gardner, and he was making a new career for himself unearthing priceless works of art that could be bought at bargain basement prices on behalf of Duveen and several other prestigious houses and sold at enormous profit. He was also writing scholarly articles and books, primarily about the art of the Italian Renaissance, and for a modest fee, confirming the provenance of purchases contemplated by his new clients.

Berenson had bought a beautiful old manor house near Florence, "I Tatti," where he lived on a very lavish scale. Unable to support his extravagant tastes with his meager income, Berenson made a pact with Duveen Brothers to give his approval to all the works procured for the gallery's millionaire patrons, to whom he disdainfully referred as "the geese who lay the golden eggs," in exchange for 25 percent of the profit involved.

But as the world economy slipped into a deep depression in 1914, many of those patrons were disinclined to dispatch their debts promptly and were delinquent in remitting their payments in a timely manner. This left the Duveens in an awkward position vis-à-vis their own debts, and they instructed Deloitte, their accountants, to hold off paying the gallery's bills for as long as possible. The situation, of course, threw Berenson into a panic. At first he groveled and whined and said he needed cash payment immediately. Then he appealed for compassion because his "stocks [were] almost unsaleable" and his bankers refused to lend him anything more. At length he became threatening, saying it would be "unwise" of Duveen not to honor his commitments, and demanding hefty monthly payments of thousands of pounds.[4]

It was at this point that he received a letter from Henry advising him of the purchase and stating, "I am now its happy owner. For years I have dreamed of living with a Fra Angelico. I always had in my imagination the kind of an example of this great master's work that I should like to live with and the possession of this picture has realized that dream."[5] He continued that his own concern was its condition and asked Berenson for his opinion. Berenson promptly replied, heaping accolades upon the painting and stating that the masterpiece not only elevated the reputation of Fra Angelico to new heights, but also represented a whole new understanding of the history of fourteenth-century Italian art. The painting cost $140,000, $80,000 in cash as down payment, with the balance payable in eight months with 6 percent interest. The only stipulation in the sales contract was a two-year guarantee against cracking or splitting.

The following winter Duveen mounted an exhibition of important Italian paintings in New York, and Henry was delighted to lend him the Fra Angelico for the occasion. Among the glowing reviews in the press there was a single exception. A young professor by the name of Richard Offner disputed the attribution of J. P. Morgan's Girlandais and suggested that Clarence Mackay's Botticelli and two

Mantegnas from the Widener collection has been created by less exalted hands. Last but not least, he questioned the authenticity of Henry's Fra Angelico. Duveen was highly incensed and wrote a personal letter to his "dear friend" Goldman that he need not be under the least apprehension. However, Duveen said he didn't understand whether the article, which ran in a minor art publication, was prompted by malice or insufficient knowledge, since a few days before the exhibition opened Offner had personally told him that he had advised Henry to buy the painting and had recommended it very highly.

Henry responded pragmatically from his summer bastion in Karlsbad, Germany, that this was true, but he did not think Offner malicious and he had confidence in the honesty of his judgment and the rectitude of his intentions. He felt that without a doubt the Fra Angelico could stand on its own merit. His only concern was the lukewarm reception given the piece by the major German art critics. Duveen wired him on the steamship *Deutschland,* which was sailing back to the United States, that he appreciated Henry's attitude, adding that he always had the greatest respect for his opinions of human nature and for the broad outlook he took on things in general.

An interoffice memo from Duveen's New York office to gallery headquarters in London a few days later reported that the distinguished British dealer Gerald Agnew would like to have a photograph of the Fra Angelico as he had a client who was very interested in buying it. Henry was not interested.

Meanwhile, Berenson reneged on his promise to write a laudatory article, citing the books he was writing, serious scholarly books that would need to be turned aside in order to write the piece. Rather than commit time to writing about the Fra Angelico, lovely as it was, he would have to ask Duveen to take it back from Henry, if necessary, and absorb any loss that was incurred. A postal snarling match ensued in which Duveen claimed he was fearful for his reputation, not any financial loss, and insisted that Berenson get him out of this embarrassing mess. It seems that Berenson, ever playing both ends against the middle, then retorted that Duveen should "tell Mr. Goldman to let anyone he likes write about his Fra Angelico."[6] He himself was not ready to do so, being deeply engaged in other work. He would consider getting around to it sometime in the future, he said, when he was not so busy. One is inclined to wonder if, with his personal security holdings plummeting, he bore a personal grudge against the esteemed erstwhile senior partner in Goldman Sachs, or if he was afraid of being caught waffling his reputation as the preeminent authority of the twenties on Renaissance art.

In 1918, fully retired from Goldman Sachs after the debacle over partisanship in the war, Henry threw himself heart and soul into acquiring art, just as he had done with the firm. He had purchased a number of $5,000 to $10,000 works from the beginning of the century, but now he had the time and the money and was gathering the know-how to collect in a far grander way. Amongst his earlier acquisitions was a series of five seventeenth-century paintings called "the Five Senses," by the Flemish artist David Teniers the Younger, whose travels had taken them from royal residences in Madrid and Paris to Surrey, England, Florence, and once again to Paris. "Seeing," the first canvas, depicts a young artist drawing a model. "Hearing" shows a bagpipe player and a peasant, singing and playing. "Tasting" shows a very merry drinker holding his drinking cup out to a servant to be refilled. In "Feeling" a man is removing a plaster from his wounded hand with an expression of great pain on his face. And "Smelling" shows a gardener carrying a pot of carnations with a woman who is obviously his mistress plucking one of the blooms. Meticulously drawn, richly colored, and full of vigor, the group was a fine example of genre painting, but they were not of the same caliber as the famous masterpieces that later caught his eye. They remained part of his collection for less than ten years, and the $25,000 they fetched when he sold them represented a minor portion of his payment for Giorgione's "Portrait of a Man" (which Berenson erroneously attributed to Titian). It was one of the few swaps ever made in his collection.

Around the same time, he purchased two early fourteenth-century examples of medieval religious art, "Madonna and Child," attributed to Bernardo Daddi, who painted the frescoes in Santa Croce in Florence, and which was much later labeled by the Italian government as a Giorgione, and the "Adoration of the Child" by Jan Van Eycks' great pupil Petrus Christus. He also acquired a fourth-century B.C. marble head of a maiden by the Greek sculptor Praxiteles, a rarity in any collection of the day. Wilhelm Valentiner, the German art scholar who catalogued the Goldman collection, was quoted as saying that this sculpture's beauty could best be detected by touch, an interesting comment considering the fact that Henry lost his sight completely just a few years after he bought it.

One of Henry's basic rules in his relationship with the house of Duveen was that all the details of his purchases be kept strictly confidential. He had bought the "Portrait of an Officer" by Franz Hals early in 1916. The famous Dutch painting, which now hangs in our National Gallery, shows a seventeenth-century cavalier, bearded and mustachioed, wearing a broad-brimmed gray hat. He is obviously enjoying life and living it to the fullest. It was only a few weeks after the portrait had taken pride of place over the living room mantelpiece in Henry's home that the Sunday edition of the *New York Herald* published a photograph of it accompanied by a précis penned by a staff writer named Boswell. Henry, in a flash of his famous fury, wrote to Duveen Brothers: "I was intensely mortified at the vulgar publication in the *Herald* on Sunday. This was the one thing that I wanted to avoid. Inasmuch as the *Herald* got a reproduction of my picture, I would thank you to find out for me how they got it. I trust not through you."[7]

In response, Duveen's disclaimed responsibility, throwing the blame on the shoulders of some unknown competitor and noting that a number of people had called at the Goldmans' apartment to see the new acquisition, which was a well-known work, prominently described and illustrated in books and catalogues on Hals's works, and therefore not a difficult subject for a journalist to research. Apologies were tendered, but the point was made. After that, only by express written permission were people other than family and personal friends allowed to view the collection, and then by appointment only. Among them, ten years later, were the wife and

Franz Hals' "Portrait of an Officer," now in the National Gallery in Washington, D.C.

daughter of Hjalmar Schacht, the German currency comptroller who became known to the world as "Hitler's banker."

The United States' entry into World War I brought the art market in the United States to a sudden halt. There were no more extravagant purchases, and sellers were tucking their prized possessions away for a rainy day. The minds and hearts of the world were riveted on the action at the front and the brave souls who thought they were bringing peace to the world for eternity. But soon after the armistice the press reported Henry's purchase of a valuable Van Dyck for quite a large sum. This ran contrary to the general state of affairs in the art market. In 1920 Duveen remarked to Henry in a letter that the psychological panic of the general public in New York was having a terrible effect on the art market. No one wanted to sell in bad times, and there was nothing worthy of consideration being offered either privately or in the galleries.

Henry responded from Berlin, where he had spent six "very interesting weeks" in conferences with "the big interests," including President Hindenburg, Hans Luther (president of the Reichsbank at that time), and Chancellor Heinrich Brüning, who had been appointed to stabilize the economic crisis that was tearing the young Weimar Republic to shreds. He cautioned that conditions could not well be much worse, but felt successful men of business should conserve their credit and keep their flags flying. Duveen's stock in trade, he said, was magnificent and required no replenishing. But he must sign off now, as he was to have a private luncheon with the president. To his surprise, Henry was told over coffee that he was to be given honorary German citizenship in return for the advice and aid he had so assiduously given to the country.

Correspondence between Duveen and Henry bounced back and forth between continents almost every week. They delighted in sharing each other's thoughts, and what had once been a formal, professional tone in their letters became increasingly personal. Duveen would tell Henry about the latest doings on "the Rialto," what they were eyeing and buying in London and Paris and New York, and Henry would return the favor by reporting on the world of German politics and economics as well as what was on the block in Berlin, Karlsbad, Baden, St. Moritz. As Henry's poor eyesight worsened and he embarked on a long series of optical operations, Duveen became an increasingly involved friend and made certain the two could rendezvous for long gossipy chats over coffee and cigars at New York's St. Regis or the Paris Ritz as frequently as possible. He even arranged to have identical apartments, one above the other, reserved at the Claridge Hotel in London so they could share their free time together. The Duveen suite, of course, was always beautifully decorated with the newest things he had for sale, just in case some prospect should drop by to say hello.

By the spring of 1921, the titled aristocrats in Great Britain were still feeling the economic pinch that followed the armistice, sufficiently so that many were divesting themselves of family heirlooms piece by piece. And so it happened that a particularly lovely sixteenth-century bronze inkwell by the Florentine sculptor and goldsmith Benvenuto Cellini fell into the hands of Duveen Brothers. Purchased from A. H. Godfrey, of Brooke House in Cambridge, this

Henry's beloved Cellini inkstand

seventeen-inch gem, which the artist labeled "Virtue Conquering Vice," was a finely chiseled and hammered figure of a nude female holding a club standing on a prostrate evil old woman with a gorgon's head and flowing hair. It was covered in dark brown lacquer. The provenance was impeccable, having been in the possession of the same family for many generations. The heir described them as serious amateur connoisseurs, not "globe trotting collectors," who had at one time been antiquities consultants to the Italian Ministry.

Duveen was thrilled to acquire such a treasure, knowing that he would have no problem reselling it at a substantial profit. But always alert to the possibility of false claims, he sent it by messenger to the director of the Kaiser Friedrich Museum in Charlottenburg, Germany, for authentication. The director, Dr. Wilhelm von Bode, a delightful old fellow who was close to Henry, recalled the piece from the time when it was still in the Palazzo Borghese, and after exhaustive examination compared it with an almost identical rendition in Vienna belonging to Adolphe de Rothschild. He had not the slightest doubt that the bronze was an original by Cellini and that it must have been very celebrated, although the base differed from the Rothschild inkwell in a number of details.

In a casual little note sent to Baden-Baden, where Henry was having a streak of luck at the gaming tables and Babette was taking her annual cure, Duveen dangled the Cellini temptingly. He would never have been crass enough to make a direct sales pitch, but couldn't resist describing it as "one of the finest bronzes in the world."[8] He realized, he wrote, that it was hardly a propitious time to be buying fine art, but he assured Henry that it was reserved for him whenever he felt the time was right. It remained on Henry's desk at home until 1938, when the apartment at 998 Fifth Avenue was cleared posthumously, and Babette moved to sumptuous quarters at the Hotel Pierre.

Although Duveen was undoubtedly disappointed not to be the purveyor of the "ravishing Donatello" Henry purchased from a London dealer later that year, he bided his time. He was confident that Henry would be making plenty of future acquisitions through Duveen's and he was shrewd enough to compliment Henry on whatever he acquired elsewhere. He even offered to give those pieces safe harbor at his New York galleries until the Goldmans returned from their lengthy European sojourns.

The Donatello "Madonna and Child," which he said he himself would have bought had Henry not preempted him, was a special case in point. The seller had asked ten thousand pounds for it, just a little more than Duveen was prepared to pay. In a letter he joked with Henry about his not needing any advice on trading.[9] Nearly life sized, the Madonna was sculpted of terra-cotta and was a particularly warm, human vision of the Virgin. Her costume is traditional: a red gown and a long gold-bordered light blue mantle that falls to the ground in heavy folds. Her hair is covered with a white veil fastened around her forehead with a white ribbon that is decorated with small blue and red stars and a red border. The child is snuggled up next to her breast, sucking his thumb, and looks like an adorable cherub. The piece came from a private chapel in one of the palaces belonging to the Pazzi family in Florence. Acknowledged to be the greatest sculptor of the early Renaissance in Italy, Donatello was known for his work on the cathedral, the campanile, and San Michele, as well as commissions for private families such as the Medici. The work had never before traveled far from home, but never had she been so devotedly adored. Henry called her "a perfect dream."

The Goldman children saw little of their parents in the ensuing five years. Florence and Edwin Vogel's daughter Betsy had started school; she was a shy girl, somewhat awkward and lacking in self-esteem. Robert and his second wife, Mildred, produced a boy and a girl in the few years they were married, and Henry Jr., known as "Junie," after spending a year studying banking in Paris at his father's behest, married pretty Adrienne Straus, a New York debutante once pursued by his elder brother. Henry and Babette lived the life of fabulous gypsies in the capitals of Europe, enriching their knowledge of paintings and sculpture and music while Henry conferred with the top brass in finance on how to stabilize the German currency and stem the raging inflation. Babette attended many of the high-end auctions in Paris, London, and Rome, often in the company of one of Duveen's minions, purchasing valuable French, Italian, and Flemish antiquities with a shrewd and perceptive eye and was befriended by most of the leading lights on the cultural scene.

In the early twenties, Henry embarked on a voyage of discovery of his own. As the bells of the Madeleine and Notre Dame welcomed in the New Year, he wrote to Duveen from the Hotel Ritz. "I have been in Paris two weeks and excepting Mondays when it is closed for cleaning, and on Christmas day when it did not open, I spent every day at the Louvre with Valentiner until they put me out. What a treasure house it is!" He went on to say that he had been over to see the gallery's "marvelous Titian . . . three times. . . . It is simply bewitching,"[10] and that he was "perfectly gone on it. Holy God," he wrote, "I would like to own that picture but I know it is beyond me, especially in these times. It is one of the few nudes that is so aesthetic that it lends itself admirably to a private collection." He was, of course, referring to what became Babette's favorite, "The Toilet of Venus," which had been hidden in private European collections for almost four centuries and which clearly inspired Renoir and Pisarro in their use of color and light.

Prior to framing a response to such bubbling enthusiasm, Duveen had received a secret report from his representatives in Paris that related that Henry and Babette had been in several times to see "the Titian" and that Henry was very excited about it.[11] He said he had also been to see the one at the Louvre and that he considered the one at Duveen's much finer. He was hoping when he returned home, he said, to make enough money to be able to buy it, but that things in America were really very bad, that no one had any money. He did not ask the price nor did the gallery quote him one, but he inquired if it had cost Duveen's a lot of money, and he was told that they had paid a large sum for it. It was more than likely, the gallery said, that if Morgan (who was Duveen's biggest client at the time) took a pass, Henry would buy the picture if it was within his means. He was crying very poor at this time.

Henry and Joe circled one another verbally like a couple of horse traders about the painting. Sly as the proverbial fox, Joe told Henry how glad he was that he liked the Titian. He agreed that it was a

Henry found Titian's "Toilet of Venus" simply bewitching

perfect gem and complimented Henry's taste and perspicacity in wanting to own it. He claimed that, along with many other fine things, he was going to just lock it away and not show it to any prospective buyers until the depression had run its course. When

Henry asked the price, Duveen quoted $195,000 and made it clear that he would brook no negotiation.

The bill of sale for the painting, complete with the provenance dating back to a sixteenth-century noble family of Ferrara, is dated six months later. The purchase price was $135,000, payable in three installments: $25,000 down, $50,000 in eight months, and $60,000 eight months after that, with the installments paying 6 percent interest. It appears that this was one of the rare times when Duveen was outmaneuvered and still remained on friendly terms with a client.

The years between 1921 and 1925 were possibly the most exciting in Henry's life, and from the standpoint of his health, the most troublesome. He went on a spending spree, buying sixteenth-century Renaissance masterpieces by Masolino, as well as baroque canvases by Rubens and Van Dyck. Many of his acquisitions were eagerly pursued by would-be buyers for years, but Henry refused and adamantly stuck to his decision. As he wrote to Duveen from Germany, "Your remarks about the enhancement of the value of my collection are undoubtedly correct but inasmuch as I will part with nothing so long as I live, this is a paper satisfaction. When the war was on and when in consequence the great shifting of wealth in Europe was taking place, I bent all my energies to collecting, and I agree that I did well in this. You know, my dear Joe, I was not as stupid as I looked while I was acquiring."[12]

The painting in question, "Meleager Offering the Head of the Boar of Calcydon to Atalanta," is a large and very powerful painting, earthy, primitive and lusty, and astonishing in its use of color.

The brushwork and the luminous rendition of the flesh are among the finest of the artist's work. It depicts a well-known episode in the *Iliad* in which the son of Aeneas, one of the most illustrious warriors of his day, kills a monstrous boar that has ravaged a small town in Aetolia and presents its severed head to a beautiful goddess, Atalanta. The painting had been bought from the estate of Rodolphe Kann, a famous art aficionado in Paris, and hangs today in New York's Metropolitan Museum of Art.

But meanwhile, Henry's eyesight was deteriorating more and more rapidly. He had trouble distinguishing the varied shades of red in the clothing of the Madonna in his Van Dyck masterpiece, or the shadowed figure of Alfonso d'Este in "The Toilet of Venus." No longer could he revel in the colors of a rainbow or the glint of the sun on the copper rooftops of New York's skyline. Everything seemed to be in shadow. Specialists at Lenox Hill Hospital recommended what became the first of a number of surgeries to improve the situation.

While Henry was hospitalized for the procedure Babette, at Duveen's urging, arranged for a complete makeover of the 998 Fifth Avenue living room so that the growing collection of paintings would be more appropriately displayed. From then on it was referred to as "the Italian room" and was hung with gold silk wall coverings. There were gleaming parquet floors, Aubusson rugs, ormolu andirons, Florentine tables, and armchairs upholstered with Babette's fine petit point, and last, but not least, a big black Steinway grand piano with a fabulous tone, selected after many had been tested by noted artists Rosina Lhevinne and Wanda Landowska. Duveen himself oversaw the cleaning and hanging of all the paintings and ordered Sèvres vases filled with yellow roses, Babette's favorites, when the job was finished.

Babette was so delighted with the result that she commissioned Duveen's team to overhaul the gallery where the sculptures were displayed, which was adjacent to the little entrance vestibule. The sapphire blue walls and judiciously placed overhead spotlights, installed under the watchful eye of a prominent theatrical lighting designer, focused dramatically on the Della Robbia "Madonna and Child Surrounded by Angels" hanging across from the entryway above the spot where the Goldmans traditionally placed their white-flocked Christmas tree.

Henry delighted in hearing Duveen's backstage stories of the art world almost as much as Joe enjoyed pulling off a coup. Facing yet another eye surgery, he took vicarious pleasure in the lifeline Duveen threw out, connecting him to the latest foibles of the big collectors.

In return, Henry would update him on the vagaries of the stock market and economic conditions at home and abroad. He also questioned why it was suddenly "raining Titians" when they had formerly been so hard to come by. He reported that his eye problems were even more severe than he had been led to believe and that he had stayed in Berlin for six long weeks, enduring a "more or less trying time," undergoing three procedures on his right eye that had tired him very much. "It looks as though I might have to stay about that much longer before I am free to do as I please," he wrote. "During all this time I have been confined to my rooms but physically and spiritually, barring occasional blues and perhaps a little homesickness for you, I am perfectly well. I do miss our frequent afternoon chats." He added that Babette had left him the previous evening for a short jaunt to Paris in order to attend to "some important transactions on the Rue de la Paix," which was the center of fashion at the time. "I have many interesting friends here who see me often so that time passes pleasantly," he concluded with the voice of an aging and rather lonely man.[13]

Joe Duveen, always upbeat, responded that he was confident the results of the operations would be worth the awful waiting and discomfort. As for the Titians? He thought still more would surface, as the artist had led such a long life and there was increasingly great knowledge and recognition of this master. He closed with some tidbits about his own recent purchases, a stunning Van Dyck portrait and a "real Giorgione, passed by Berenson," as well as "The Standard Bearer" by Raphael (the only Raphael in the country!), which he had bought from the Gould estate and intended to sell to Jules Bache. And then there was the news that he had decided to speculate on some real estate in southern California that purportedly was on the brink of development. It cost close to a million dollars and, against the advice of his accountants, he had bought it and mortgaged it to the hilt.

Unlike the great art collections that Duveen bought "en bloc" in Europe and patiently locked away for piecemeal future sales that netted him huge gains, real estate was a different kind of wager. His timing was poor, and the strategy didn't work out. He was stuck with hefty monthly payments and zero return. To add to his woes, there was a great shortage of quality paintings on the market in

1927, and many of his clients were haggling and delaying payment on their expensive hobby.

Henry's warm letter of sympathy upon the death of one of Duveen's best clients advised his friend to get rid of the land he had bought in California—the client had been a real estate pro with great knowledge of the area, Joe was not—pay off the mortgage and whatever debts he owed, and invest the remaining proceeds judiciously. He, Henry, would recommend buying two thousand shares of Commercial Investment Trust (later known as CIT Financial Corporation) which paid good dividends and, as the prime lender in the booming automobile industry, stood to rise in value significantly. He added that this was the largest single investment that he and his wife held, and that he was "notoriously cautious and not one to take any flyers."

Duveen, of course, was highly appreciative of Henry's financial guidance and, revealing a shift in the nature of their relationship, began to confide in him the details of all his major transactions and to look for Goldman's assistance in investing the very sizable profits of his company. (Evidently Duveen's appreciation of his guidance was not shared by everyone at his firm. A memo in the gallery's files under the heading "Re Mr. Goldman" read, "Merely because we furnished him with so much intimate information about our business affairs heretofore, he is practically asking for up to date information about our business. It is essential that we keep details of our business to ourselves.") He happily reported that he had sold a number of "very fine things to Mellon, including a Franz Hals and a Titian," and that he had left some other very valuable paintings on approval with him, which he appraised at well over a million dollars. There was a great Rembrandt portrait of a man, a Velasquez portrait, a Rubens, and yet another Titian. He had agreed to sell them as a lot, and Mellon said he would not haggle on the price any further. Duveen was more than delighted with the deal. It would give him the best year of his career, even if a few of the pieces fell through the cracks.

Henry was both pleased and flattered to be asked for advice about Duveen's investments. He modestly wrote: "I can, of course, give you only the best there is in me and the benefit of my own personal experience, which I am happy to say has been successful."[14] The recommended portfolio consisted of about half old and tested industrial stocks and half bonds, all companies in which Henry had invested for himself, reliable and with long-term potential and attractive dividends. They included American Tobacco, U.S. Steel, May Department Stores, the Pullman Company, and a basket of high-grade railroad securities. In the following eighteen months he would add AT&T, Consolidated Can, Westinghouse Electric, and Woolworth, each of which rose a minimum of 50 percent in the following year. He also praised Duveen's improved attitude toward new clients, those who were buying in the $100,000 class. "The big guns are old and will always be the ones on whom you will make your big money, but wide distribution will be very important in the long run," he said. "The new fellows are usually young and are likely to become big."[15] Among them were Henry's daughter Florence and her husband, Ed Vogel, who were picking up first-rate Renoirs and Van Goghs at very reasonable prices in Paris. Neither Joe nor Henry thought they had much of a future.

Six months later, Henry was again in Germany and received an autographed catalogue of a major exhibition of Italian paintings Duveen Brothers had launched in New York. "I had the whole catalogue read to me last night," he wrote in thanks. "Knowing every picture there is in it, I could visualize the whole book splendidly in my mind." He had been assured that he was making progress with his vision and was looking forward to undergoing a major procedure the following January. It would, the specialists promised, take care of everything. But right now he was missing Babette, who had left earlier in the day for a cure at Karlsbad and then planned a week or two of after cure. Perhaps Elena Gerhardt and "another friend" would join her there. "I have become increasingly dependent on her," he admitted. "She takes care of me in every way."

In her absence, he concentrated ever more keenly on business and foresaw that economic recovery would be very slow indeed, much slower than the newspapers indicated. Believing that the carefree spending days of the Coolidge administration were winding down, he cautioned, "My dear Joe, let me give you a little advice for the next season. I think the U.S. is in an industrial commercial reaction which will not blow over quite as quickly as the big interests and the press which they control would have us believe. I would therefore advise you not to be very aggressive in buying and to acquire . . . only epoch making things . . . and keep them dark if I had to. You did absolutely right in not buying any securities this spring. This is a good time to keep very strong for the purposes of your legitimate business. While reports from America are not good I feel easy of mind in the consciousness that all my securities are first class and you ought to feel the same way. Temporary fluctuations do not interest me."[16]

Duveen's next letter told of purchasing a rare Vermeer "Portrait of a Woman." Joe thought it a great find, particularly since his old adversaries from Knoedler's arrived twenty-four hours later expecting to buy it. "This is exactly what I expected," he crowed. "Duveen Brothers are always twenty-four hours earlier!"[17] And, he continued, Goldman Sachs & Co. were just as much on the alert when "a certain great gentleman was on the spot. I know you don't like flattery, but I am constantly hearing from prominent men downtown that Goldman Sachs is not at all top drawer today. People say that their way of doing business is not totally on the up-and-up."

Henry received this news with mixed emotions. "I am, of course, egotistical enough to be glad if it is true that I am missed," he said, "but I am equally sorry that a great old name, which I did so much to build up, is on the toboggan." And then he warned his friend to "play the game coyly" in the season to come. "Be cautious," he repeated over and over, "general business is slowly going to let up. You cannot look for as much buying power in America in the coming year as you found in the last. Even the rich will make less and consequently will want to spend less. There is possible business disturbance ahead. . . . Obviously if any great works of art appear on the market you will want to get your hands upon them, but there is a difference between looking for them aggressively and letting them come along."[18] It was the same advice he gave to his children in those months just before the crash of 1929.

It wasn't the cataclysmic upheaval of the stock market alone that roiled the fine art market so drastically as the new decade was born. As Henry observed, "Economically the Germans are very bad indeed, and politics are so involved there as to be difficult to grasp." The National Socialist party had swept into power and the man in the street welcomed Hitler's installation as the new chancellor as a cure for the 30 percent unemployment that ravaged the country and the currency crisis that had literally wiped out the middle class. Much of the blame for the dreadful economic situation was focused squarely on the German-Jewish bankers and the corporations that had close ties to them, such as the chemical giant I. G. Farben. Anti-Semitism ran rife.

Although, to begin with, wealthy Germans laughed at the Nazis and considered them contemptible socialist boors, the proletariat was more easily swayed. The Goldmans, visiting with their friends among the intelligentsia as they did every spring, were certain that the regime was just a passing fad and would soon blow away. Their primary concern was that the promised results of Henry's many surgeries had not materialized, and by then he had only 10 percent of his vision. He had become more and more reliant on Babette and had retained the services of a graduate student to read and write for him and a full-time caregiver to spell Babette when she went on her little sabbaticals. A young German-American woman, single and not unattractive, Frieda Schulz, known to everyone as "Schulzie," was a perfect choice: bright, even-tempered, devoid of family ties. Like Gene Scheck, the Goldman chauffeur, she was thought of as "family" and not hired help.

Henry's view of the sociopolitical situation in Germany did a total about-face in 1933. He wrote Joe from the Hotel Adlon in Berlin, "I am suffering tortures studying and seeing what they are doing to our people here." He had sent Babette to Paris and planned to get together with her in London a week or so later. Meanwhile, he was observing cemetery desecrations, brownshirt beatings, and old people taunted in the street whenever he walked out the hotel door. The government started a boycott of Jewish-owned stores and posted uniformed guards with swastikas outside their doors. People with whom Henry had socialized for years crossed the street and peered into vacant shop windows to avoid talking to him.

"It is unbelievable that Hitler could ever become the leader of such a cultured creative country," he wrote. But he had not been alone in his reluctance to accept reality. By the time they opened their eyes, even affluent Jewish families were deprived of their possessions, forbidden to attend museums and concerts and movies, not permitted to have servants or radios or telephones, and finally, forced to leave their homes. But while Jews were being removed from their teaching positions at universities, and "non-Aryan" books were torn from library shelves, no one foresaw the impending confiscation of so much great art. Some of the major collectors were able to sell their treasures and get out of the country before all the walls came tumbling down. Some buried them in their backyards, in depots, castle keeps, and museum storerooms, or smuggled them to Switzerland. The vast majority of the priceless collections became part of Goering's hoard, some of which is still in the process of being returned to the rightful owners and their heirs. When Henry left Germany that spring, he could never have imagined that it would be for the last time, yet he began to harbor concern regarding the fate of his own beloved art collection when he eventually passed away.

Over the years, Babette had privately harbored doubts about Duveen's sincerity in his relationship with her husband. She found him erudite and amusing and was appreciative of the vast amounts of time he lavished on Henry, but she always had a nagging suspicion that much of the cozy "noodling" was little more than a façade laid over a skeleton of pure commercialism. All that was laid to rest on the occasion of Henry's seventy-eighth birthday, when she decided to fete him with an old-fashioned barbecue dinner in the elegant Fifth Avenue apartment. The Sheraton dining room furniture was cleared out to make room for long wooden picnic tables and rustic benches like the ones at Bull Point Camp, the Goldmans' summer retreat. Red checkered tablecloths were produced, red and white roses, and lots of fat red candles. There was an accordionist, and a little platform had been erected at one end of the room where roasts and toasts were to be performed. It was a total surprise for the black-tied attendees, who sipped vintage champagne with their hamburgers and drank "eiskaffee," a German treat of iced coffee mixed with ice cream, with the birthday cake.

The Duveens, as usual, were late. Very late. They arrived, in fact, as the grandchildren were serenading the guest of honor with his favorite selection of German folk songs and a hearty chorus of "Happy Birthday." Forgoing his usual wild praise—"These are the finest! never seen anything like 'em before!"—Joe presented his old friend with a blue box. Inside there rested two fine miniature portraits by

Holbein that Henry had long admired. Unable to see them, Henry ran his fingers over and over their features with a loving touch. The party grew very quiet for a few moments. Even the children were extremely moved.

Next August, 1936, Joe was in London and received a letter from Henry's summer residence on Upper Saranac Lake. "Here in America," Henry wrote, "conditions are developing and continuing to improve exactly as I had thought they would, and if the President [Roosevelt], whose policies are largely responsible for the improvement, is reelected, I think the upward movement will continue. If, however, he should be defeated, I think the applecart will be upset and in that event you merchants will have to be prepared for a backslide."[19] He begged for more information about the headway Joe was making with Mellon in developing a National Gallery of Art in the nation's capital, and then remarked that he was giving serious thought to the sale of his entire art collection, either by private sale, which he preferred, or if necessary, at auction. "In a month from now I enter my eightieth year," he said, "and I have a strange desire to get my house in order for the grand finale of all mortal beings. I want to act while I am still possessed of all my mental vigor." He never discussed the matter with his family and suggested Duveen help him dispose of everything with some dispatch.

Joe, confidant and chum, but always the consummate huckster, wasted no time contacting one of his most important clients, Samuel Kress, whose collection had already surpassed even Mellon's in size and scope, and asked him to put in a bid. According to Meryle Secrest, Duveen's biographer, Kress was astonished. "Is he broke?"[20]

he exclaimed, that being the only reason he considered justification for selling a picture. Kress was informed by the secretary who had brought him the news that the offer had nothing to do with insolvency, but that he would have to make up his mind in a hurry—that very afternoon, in fact. Henry Goldman was a man of little patience. "Hold Goldman off!" said Kress, disregarding the advice. By the time his representative accessed a telephone to try to delay negotiations, it was too late. Henry's lifelong insistence on promptness had not changed. He had sold ten of his most important paintings in bulk to Duveen for a lump sum of $775,000, considerably below their insured value.

It was a supreme gesture of friendship, as Joe could now place his own evaluations on the separate pieces rather than buy them at auction, where the prices would be on public record, and would then be difficult to turn over advantageously. Kress, meanwhile, was convinced that he had missed out on a very important acquisition and demanded to see the pictures. Duveen was only too glad to display Henry's masterpieces in Kress's apartment, along with a typical stream of superlatives. Although his advisors suggested the old man exercise caution and voiced the opinion that certain pieces had been over restored, Kress bought the entire lot, quite likely because they now had the added cachet of being "Duveens," which added considerably to their value.

The balance of Henry's treasures were sold soon afterward by Duveen's at fixed prices set by the gallery. Should the items sell for more than the specified prices, Duveen's was to retain the excess. If they sold for less, Duveen's would make up the difference. It was a very attractive arrangement for the gallery, which quoted reserves well below their insured valuations, an act that was advantageous to the tax liabilities of the Goldman estate as well.

But one would rather believe that it was part of a grand altruistic plan, conceived over coffee and cigars one afternoon at the St. Regis Hotel, to make these beautiful objects, hidden away for years in a private collection, available to everyone. "The Toilet of Venus" now hangs in London's National Gallery and Franz Hals's "Portrait of an Officer" graces the National Gallery of Art in Washington, D.C. Rubens's "Meleager" was a bequest to the Metropolitan Museum of Art. The treasured Rembrandt was sold by Duveen's to the Wildenstein Gallery in 1947 and remained there for five years until it was purchased by the Putnam Foundation, which gave it to the Timken Museum of Art in San Diego, California.

CHAPTER EIGHT

Bull Point Camp

*H*enry and Babette purchased Bull Point Camp in 1914 from financier Otto Kahn for a summer home. Marcus had passed away a few years earlier, and in his will he had left his mansion on the Jersey Shore to his daughter Louisa and her husband, Sam, with whom he had lived in his final years. Henry's family had traditionally spent their summer vacations at Elberon, but now the five-minute stroll from one house to the other put them just a bit too close for comfort, considering that the brothers-in-law did not share the warmest of relations.

Babette, concerned by repeated warnings in the newspapers of U-boat attacks on unarmed U.S. vessels sailing the Atlantic, used all her wiles to dissuade Henry from making his usual spring trip to the continent. As an alternative, she had suggested they purchase a vacation home, a Great Camp, in the Adirondack Mountains where they could entertain family and special friends during the month of August. The location they chose was in a spectacular wooded wilderness preserve. Upper Saranac Lake had been primarily a logging and iron mining enclave until the last years of the Gilded Age, when train service linked it to urban centers. Wealthy families like the Rockefellers and Lehmans were attracted to the clean, fresh air, the abundance of trout in the lakes, mountains as far as the eye could see, and especially the privacy and solitude one could find, quite surprisingly, not that far from New York.

Henry thought it was an added plus that his brother Julius, with whom he had remained close, had built a vacation home in nearby Keene Valley. Julius's wife, Sarah, was the daughter of Felix Adler, the social reformist who founded the Ethical Culture movement in New York City. Adler had established a retreat there many years earlier and was part of a circle of theologians, including Henry Sloane Coffin, of New York's Madison Avenue Presbyterian Church, who had settled there and enjoyed interdisciplinary discussions on philosophy, morals, and religion. The Adler children were encouraged to become involved and undoubtedly influenced their future in-laws in their decision to assimilate and become, in their vernacular, "Christianized." It is unlikely that Henry was aware that his sister Rosa and her husband, Julius Sachs, were planning to build in the area, too, as were Sam and Louisa and their son Paul and his family. The growing disaffection between himself and the Sachses, and the lack of paved public roads, meant the two family compounds, located only forty-one miles from each other, might as well have been separated by the Valley of the Moon.

Although they were located in the same gorgeous swath of natural forest preserve, Keene Valley differed enormously from Saranac Lake. Landlocked, surrounded by magnificent mountain views, Keene was more thickly populated and less exclusive, and had been a magnet for intellectuals—philosophers, academics, writers such as Ralph Waldo Emerson and William James, and artists of the Hudson River School—since early in the nineteenth century. Saranac, untapped as an exclusive summer retreat until the introduction of railroad service, had the lakes, the so-called Great Camps on huge tracts of land, and the millionaires. It was here that Henry unearthed a sanctuary where, for the first time in his life, there was no need to separate his private life from his public face.

If you've had a place like Bull Point Camp in your past, you never fully shake it from your bones. It becomes a part of the fabric of your life and you remember how the family gathered there in summer, putting aside their differences for a little while and creating a fragile façade of family unity. For six weeks of the year, Bull Point was the backdrop for a great big house party, a magic circle of sisters and cousins, children and grandchildren, and talented friends from New York and abroad, who Granny's camera "snapped unawares" on the croquet or tennis court or dipping their oars in the shimmering lake.

The camp, low-key yet luxurious, was designed in the spirit of the great old English country estates and could easily accommodate several dozen guests at a time. The four-thousand-acre Adolph Lewisohn Camp, which had reportedly cost over $2 million to build, lay on one side of it, and the historic Wawbeek Inn on the other. No one could ever have referred to a stay at Bull Point Camp as "roughing it." Celebrities as varied as Sigmund Freud, Albert Einstein, Helen Keller, Queen Marie of Romania, and the great violinist Fritz Kreisler were among those who came to visit over the years, and later the children of friends in Germany who had been miraculously spirited to safety as the Hitler regime became increasingly omnipotent and brutal, would become guests.

My earliest memories of Bull Point go back to when I was five or six. My brother Peter was four years older, and Hank (Henry III) was yet to be born. There was always a feverish sense of anticipation when we prepared to go to "the mountains" in August. We held our noses and put up with the ritual dose of milk of magnesia spooned out by our mother before heading to New York's Grand Central Station to board the overnight train. Junie, our father, always insisted that we get there an hour before the gates to the track were opened, so we sat on our suitcases in the silent ten o'clock gloom, reading comic books, which were normally forbidden. When at last we were able to board, my brother and I felt like glamorous movie stars as a porter led us to a compartment all our own. To my enormous relief, Peter was quick to claim the upper berth, which looked like a dry-docked canoe when it was pulled out of its nest high up on the wall. My fräulein, Miss Weber, and Hank Walter, the strapping Columbia Law School student who had been engaged as Peter's companion for the summer, would follow a day or two later.

As the train rumbled through Harlem and then the darkened countryside, we were rocked into a dreamless sleep until there was a sudden jolt and the conductor shouted "Utica! Utica!" I raised the window shade next to my berth just a little to get a glimpse of this magical place where the train changed tracks and engines. It may not have been Paris or Rome, but for me it was the exciting gateway to the promised land—Utica, New York.

We arrived at the Saranac Inn station, the end of the line, very early the next morning and were piled into my grandfather's big electric launch, the *Babette,* which was tied up at the hotel dock. George Hoey, the fatherly, mustachioed captain who had "come with the camp," had the ship's mahogany decks gleaming, her brass fittings polished to the nines, her moss green cushions freshly plumped. Once he had made certain all our luggage was removed from the train's baggage compartment and safely secured in the Bull Point jitney, he cast off and ferried us across the lake.

As the morning mist lifted and a rainbow peeped out from behind the mountains surrounding us on every side, dozens of small, densely forested islands came into view. The inky depths of the lake turned into a shining mirror for the pines and leafy birch trees lining the shore, and George pointed out elk and badgers in the woods, and many varieties of songbirds we had never seen before. And it was quiet, so quiet. When we returned to New York in the autumn, the sound of city buses on the streets below our windows seemed deafening by comparison. Embraced by such peace and tranquility, one would never know that a great depression was rocking the country, that men were selling apples on the street corners and stuffing their jackets with newspapers to keep warm, or that the president had to summon the armed forces to protect him in the White House. Secure and serene, my grandparents had created a utopian world for those they held dearest, stopping the clock of history for a moment in time.

We arrived at the boathouse, undoubtedly the fanciest back door in existence, in half an hour's time. It was much grander than the modest gate fashioned of crisscrossed logs that fronted the brand-new state road leading all the way to Canada. That was mainly used by delivery wagons or, in winter, sleighs. The building served as a garage for Grandpa's little fleet of boats, which were more than just valuable collectibles; they were the most reliable means of transportation for visitors, mail, and groceries coming from town. Inside, there were berths for speedboats of varying sizes, and a number of rowboats and canoes were stowed on wooden rafters above. Arthur Seltzer, the caretaker and fishing guide—"I'm not a guide," he insisted, "I just take people fishing"—hauled them down almost every morning for guests to go angling and drifting and dreaming, and every once in a while, they were used for a portage from Raquette Lake to Ausable Chasm, or a hotly contested canoe tilting competition.

Upstairs were the "Bachelor Officers Quarters" where unattached friends of my father and Uncle Robert and buddies of my "Joe Prep" cousin Louis slept, along with Hank Walter; Donald Kaufman, the shy grown-up son of my Aunt Florence K., a butter and egg salesman with a lisp who plotted the annual treasure hunts that challenged all comers; and Doctor Brodnitz, the Austrian Ph.D. who had served as my grandfather's reader ever since he lost his eyesight. Poor Brodnitz, with his Continental beret and effete mannerisms, was constantly victimized by Hank and Lou and his college cronies. They even tucked a canoe in his bed one summer, and then razzed him unmercifully at the dinner table by asking, "Canoe please pass me the butter?" "Canoe play tennis tomorrow?" Granny and Grandpa remained blissfully unaware of the hazing, for they would

never have countenanced inflicting such painful humiliations on anyone, even in the guise of fun.

The main house was three stories high and imposing. It was built
in the sophisticated style of an English Tudor country house, complete with half-timbered walls, projecting gables, and brick chimneys.[1] The first floor and extensive porches, where the ladies sat in
rocking chairs and worked on their needlepoint, were fashioned of
unpeeled logs. Long, covered log walkways connected it to the
casino, the boathouse, and the aerie overlooking the "pool" enclo-
sure of the lake where the children learned to swim.

The heart of the layout was the casino, a hexagonal two-story
building where the family and their guests gathered for meals in the
first-floor dining room and then repaired to the second-floor playroom where every possible amusement could be found. Antlered
stags' heads were mounted on the wood-paneled walls, and incredibly soft polar bear rugs covered the floor. Big bay windows overlooked the lake, and a great fireplace was stacked with wood for
chilly evenings. There was a pool table, a grand piano on a small
raised stage, a Ping-Pong table and a green baize-covered poker table
ready for action. And there were books everywhere, *Alice in Won-
derland* and *Grimm's Fairy Tales* rubbing shoulders with scholarly
tomes on physics, archaeology, German art, and history. The entire
camp, with its boats and tennis court, croquet field, and miles of
forested walking paths, had the aura of a five-star hotel, but without the ostentation—or the bills.

Florence and Robert and my father, Junie, the Goldman children,
were each assigned one of the generously sized cottages scattered

throughout the property for the use of their families. The cottages were identical architecturally, sophisticated log cabins, all on one floor. Each was secluded in its grove of piney woods and featured a living room with a large stone fireplace, four bedrooms, and two knotty pine bathrooms with claw-foot tubs and huge built-in medicine chests. They were decorated with a mélange of Indian rugs, Austrian featherbeds, and fat needlepoint pillows filled with sweet-smelling balsam needles, creating an atmosphere that made every visitor feel instantly at home. Mounted near the front door was a cuckoo clock, one of my grandmother's few bows to pure German kitsch (we nicknamed ours "Little Willy"), and hidden under the living room window seat were sketch pads and watercolors, tin soldiers and board games and little birch bark canoes, purchased from Mohican Indians who trekked from camp to camp selling handicrafts every year.

My cousin Bobsie, seated inside the closet with her knees drawn up to her chin, used to keep me company before bedtime while I took my bath. Seven years my senior, she had dark curly hair, mischievous brown eyes like her father's, and a million-dollar smile. I thought of her as my big sister and was her ardent fan. Who could have guessed that she completely lacked self-confidence and thought of herself as dispensable merchandise, unconvinced that her father felt the least bit of emotion for her or her brother Lou? In her fondest dreams she pictured him coming home from work in the evening, holding her tight, and giving her goodnight kisses.

But that was not to be. Robert, with his movie star looks and infectious giggle, turned his attention elsewhere after he was divorced from Mildred, the children's mother, and rarely spent time with "the

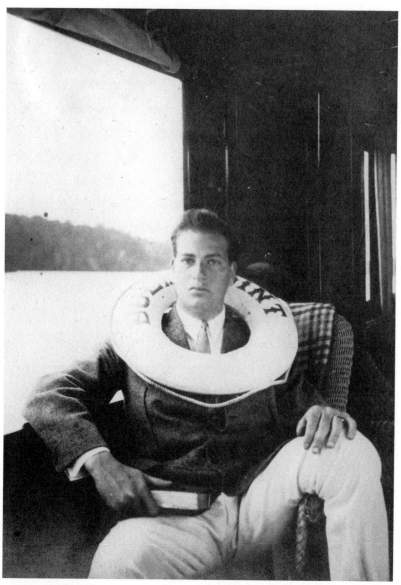

Henry Jr., known as Junie to family and friends

kiddies" except for a few weeks of court-ordered custody, when he trundled them up to his parents' home at Saranac Lake. Since childhood, he had exhibited a compulsion for collecting things, going overboard for sports cars, cameras, expensive fountain pens, and, of course, pretty women—and discarding them without remorse once he tired of them. "When I'm through, I'm through!" he would declare, as untouched by a broken marriage as he was by a misplaced cuff link or a punctured tire. But in spite of his erratic behavior, he was clearly his mother's favorite. She did not share my childish confusion when he appeared at camp with a different wife

Robert, the oft-wedded, renegade elder son

nearly every year (there were five of them), nor did his wandering eye seem to upset her, as it did Grandpa.

Betsy, the Vogels' daughter, was a generation removed from the rest of us in age. She had first been brought to Bull Point as a toddler, the only grandchild—in fact, the only child—in the charmed circle. An iconic poor little rich girl, lonely and secretive, she too had always felt rejected by her parents. She was a very minor priority in the life of Florence, so fun-loving and chatty among her friends, and Edwin, her father, a cold stuffed shirt who found children boring and disruptive. Even as an infant she and her nurse had been housed on a separate floor of the apartment building where they lived, and as soon as she reached puberty her parents began searching for a son-in-law to spirit her away. She found the wealth that set her apart from her peers an embarrassment and hated the fur coats and custom-made dresses her mother bought for her, the chauffeured Rolls-Royce that took her to school, the palatial country estate in Connecticut.

Her greatest joy lay in the world of make-believe. She loved to write and act in little plays and, as her cousins matured, she rehearsed them all month long for "The Play," which wound up the season. The script was usually composed of irreverent little satires poking fun at our grandparents and their guests. The boys all wanted to play Albert Einstein, who was so much fun to emulate with his absent-minded airs, raggedy unkempt appearance, fractured English, and enthusiasm for performing on the violin, and the girls all vied to do a number on "Granny," with her elegant wardrobe and fastidious ways. Visiting friends were enlisted as set designers, wardrobe mistresses, stagehands, and supporting members of the cast. We small fry, assured that an audience was as essential to a performance as a cast, were mollified by front-row seats next to our grandparents.

Grandpa was, of course, the undisputed king of Bull Point. And at noontime on Sundays, to make sure no one forgot it, he would toss a red velvet cape over his three-piece suit, crisp white shirt, and jaunty bow tie, and Schultzie, his caregiver, would place a papier-mâché gold crown on his head. Then the two of them would amble down to the lean-to overlooking the lake, the spot where the weekly barbecue was held. His white cane in one hand, a fat cigar in the other, he would settle into a rustic rocking chair and take out his monogrammed gold pocket watch to check the time of day. It was a unique timepiece especially crafted for the blind that charmed and entranced grownups and children alike with its musical chimes. At exactly five minutes to twelve he would rise and, with a series of trills on an old flügelhorn, summon his guests to the lunch table. And God forbid that anyone should be late! Tardiness was simply not a part of his vocabulary.

There were always at least twenty of us, and we sat at long wooden picnic tables set with red and white linens embroidered by an order of local nuns. Since the large staff was given time off to attend church services, Babette and her sisters, dressed in chic sweaters, ankle-length skirts, and high-heeled pumps, would lay out the "picnic silver," and heavy white dishes bearing the Bull Point crest, while Arthur, who was the all-around handyman as well as hunting and fishing guide, banked the fire and readied the grill. It

"The King of Bull Point"

was unheard of to suggest any variation to the menu. We had hamburgers and German-style potato salad—the kind with onions and vinegar and bacon and no mayonnaise—sliced cucumbers and tomatoes, and for dessert as many flapjacks with local maple syrup as even the growing boys could handle. When everyone had had their fill, out came the grand finale: chocolates, preferably from Maillard's, shipped every week by rail and mail boat from Paris or New York. It was the only course Grandpa could always be expected to finish.

Afterward there were word games in which even the younger children were invited to participate, and sing-alongs with my father plunking accompaniment on the mandolin and Granny's friend Elena Gerhardt leading the group in rousing choruses of "The Road to Mandalay" and old Sigmund Romberg drinking songs. And as the afternoon blossomed and the young people drifted off to their tennis matches, hikes, and sports, Grandpa would walk up to the casino for a game of bridge or backgammon with some of his guests. His favorite adversaries were his son-in-law Ed, Efrem Zimbalist's wife, Alma Gluck (a frequent guest), and his friend Henry Ittleson, the founder of the Commercial Investment Trust Company (CIT Financial), which had become one of his most lucrative investments.

The two Henrys had met in St. Louis in the 1890s, when Grandpa was low man on the totem pole in the family firm, and Ittleson (successively a minor dry goods retailer, an unsuccessful real estate agent, and a struggling stockbroker), was starting up a new business, financing receivables. By 1908, CIT counted twenty-two industrials as clients, most notably Monsanto, an agricultural giant, which had made a big splash when it entered the chemical field with the introduction of saccharin, an artificial sweetener, which they supplied to the Coca-Cola Company. In 1916, with money borrowed from Henry Goldman and department store tycoon David May, he introduced the unique concept of automobile installment financing. He started with Studebaker's four thousand dealerships and subsequently provided credit for the purchase of Hudson, Nash, and Pierce-Arrow motor cars, eventually acquiring Ford's financing arm, the Universal Credit Company. It was a revolutionary approach to marketing that helped make possible the American dream—an automobile in every garage.

The bridge games in the Bull Point casino must have been fascinating to observe, with Ittleson deaf as a post and Grandpa unable to see. Ittleson's handsome son would sit by his side and record the progress of the action on a tiny notepad while Henry's reader would identify his cards by describing them sotto voce behind a raised hand. Grandpa would then determine his strategy and instruct Brodnitz how he wished to play his hands. He had an extraordinary memory and was an intuitive, extremely competitive gambler. But he rarely won a poker game against Elena, the queen of the lieder, who was known all over Europe as a sharp player and remarkably lucky at drawing the best cards.

If Grandpa was the king of Bull Point, Granny was the unmistakable queen who coordinated all the activities, supervised the housekeeping, kept the books, ordered supplies, and was always the consummate, gracious hostess. It is amazing to think that a woman with only the equivalent of a high school education, married at the

"The Ladies League"—Babette, daughter Florence, Rosie, and Elena Gerhardt

age of nineteen at a time when women had yet to gain the vote, and who wore ankle-length skirts and mile-high hairdos, was capable of managing such a large household and holding her own in conversation with the most highly regarded artists and musicians of the day, as well as the powers that turned the wheels of fortune. But time had given her great polish and poise, and Henry's growing reliance on her had added confidence and compassion. There was a good deal more to Babette than her boundless charm and pretty face.

She was the eldest of three sisters who remained the closest of friends, regardless of the enormous gulf that separated them financially. Rose, fondly nicknamed "Roughhouse Rosie," was the good sport, always willing to hike up her skirts and wrestle with Babette's boys on the floor. She was the children's surrogate mother when their parents traveled abroad, and they loved her both for her humor and her permissiveness. When Junie suffered one of his painful mastoiditis attacks as a child and was housebound for weeks at a time, she made him soups and his favorite desserts and let him beat her at games of dominos and checkers when he became crankily fretful. She never tattled when Florence sneaked away to see a movie instead of practicing her vocal scales or, in later years, when Robert downed one too many martinis. A maiden lady, she shared her life with a longtime gentleman friend who was tied to a Catholic marriage. "Polite society" generally acknowledged their relationship, but Will was never welcome in Henry's home or invited to join the summer vacations at Bull Point. When he passed away, he and Rose had enjoyed close to fifty years as a couple, but he didn't so much as mention her in his will.

Florence Kaufman, "Aunt Florence K," the youngest sister and only twelve years older than my father, was widowed at an early age. A quiet, pretty brunette who always wore an enigmatic little smile, she and her son Donald lived in a pleasant apartment on Lexington Avenue in the seventies next door to Aunt Rosie. She frequently accompanied Babette to the Friday afternoon concerts at Carnegie Hall and was sometimes invited to join the Goldman party on their European vacations. Her personal life was always something of a mystery, although Granny and Grandpa were always trying to fix her up with one bigwig or another. When she was well into her nineties she stood in line on a frigid opening day to see *I Am Curious (Yellow),* the first hard-porn film in general release. It was never stated, but always understood, that Grandpa paid the bills for Rose and Florence, and Babette never failed to include them on Christmas Eve or the sojourns to Bull Point.

Close as the sisters may have been, even closer was Babette's relationship with singer Elena Gerhardt, who also spent the summers at Saranac after the end of World War I when her touring schedule allowed it. The Goldmans purchased a Steinway upright for her cottage so she could practice to her heart's content, and she recuperated from the stress of living in war-torn Europe by fishing, golfing, playing tennis, and joining the weekly climbs up Mount Marcy. Elena was Babette's chum, her confidante, her entree to the quasi-bohemian world of music and musicians that had captivated the older woman's imagination over the years. On the three- and four-week trips Babette took to Marienbad or Dresden or Paris, when Henry was tied up with Berlin banking affairs or recuperating in

Baden-Baden after one of his eye surgeries, it was always Elena who purportedly was her companion. People who inquired were told that the two ladies were taking the cure or attending a music festival, although one wonders whether Elena's still thriving career would have allowed such frequent and prolonged absences from the concert stage. Henry, depressed when he was left a grass widower, most likely suspected some kind of romantic dalliances, but by this time it made little difference, provided there was no scandal and the family name remained unblemished. He knew Babette had learned to love him in her own way, that she would continue to be a devoted helpmeet, and that at the end of the day he could always count on her to come back home.

Aside from her organizational skills and innate taste, Babette was clever enough to surround herself with a hand-picked staff of capable German household help, most of whom stayed with the family from the time when they first immigrated until the end of their working days. At least a dozen of them were brought to the Adirondacks to fill key positions, while locals were hired for chamber and scullery work, gardening, and clearing brush. There were three on whom she relied the most. Paul Schelin, the apple-cheeked butler who served breakfast oatmeal from a big silver chafing dish with as much panache as if it were crêpes suzettes, was so quiet that he was almost invisible. Although privy to private conversations between Henry and heads of state, universities, museums, and bastions of high finance, he maintained a discreet air of silence and a bland, nonjudgmental expression, no matter what confidences he may have overheard. His face remained expressionless when Albert Einstein enthused about "the delicious German food" at Bull Point, which he said was such a wonderful change from the bland "goy" meals he had had while visiting the Lehmans, or asked for pencil and paper to show my cousin Bobsie how to solve the problems in her summer math assignments.

Gene Scheck, the chauffeur, was tall, blond, and Nordic in appearance. He had the bearing of a military man, and the back of his neck, with which we were better acquainted than his face, was slightly pockmarked. We never saw him wearing anything except his smart black livery and could only imagine there was a full head of hair under his shiny chauffeur's cap. Our grandparents undoubtedly knew whether he had a wife and children. Certainly the rest of us did not, as he seemed to appear at an instant's notice at any hour of the day or night, kindly, soft-spoken, helpful. Among the silent tribe of uniformed men who waited patiently in the bitter cold of New York's streets in January and sweltered in the summer sun, Gene had an uncanny ability to maneuver the big, black town car to the head of the line of limousines double-parked outside the stock exchange, Carnegie Hall, or Saks. At Saranac Lake, he took great pride in driving the camp jitney, with its style-setting wood-paneled sides, broad running board, and backbreaking suspension, and the black Ford cabriolet that could accommodate eight or nine children on a run to Lake Placid to feed ice cream cones to the reputedly domesticated black bears.

Most special of all was Schultzie, Frieda Schultz, Grandpa's companion and caregiver, a forty-something German-American kindergarten teacher who applied for the position in the late twenties when jobs were difficult to find. Warm, empathetic Schultzie filled the role of secretary, nurse, dresser, and general factotum, and was an indispensable member of the family circle. It was she who indulged Henry's one personal extravagance by washing and ironing his bedsheets every day, and she who made sure he did not stumble when he insisted on joining the group on their long daily walks through the woods. She was the commentator who shared his vantage point on the grassy hill overlooking the croquet and tennis courts, describing the costumes the tournament contestants wore as well as their wickets and aces, and the personal shopper who helped him select extravagant gifts for Babette to commemorate each and every occasion. And she was his companion one chilly early morning when he waited, wrapped in blankets in his rocking chair outside the boathouse, a steaming cup of coffee in his hand, to greet Yehudi Menuhin and his father, who were coming to visit him after a separation of two long years. When Captain George Hoey cut the motor of his speedboat, the *Bobsie,* and he heard footsteps approaching the dock, Henry was so overjoyed he nearly fell in the lake.

CHAPTER NINE

A Child Prodigy

The relationship of the fabulously gifted young violinist Yehudi Menuhin and the blind old financier had its beginnings just a few weeks after Black Thursday, the day of the great stock market crash of 1929, which signaled the beginning of the Great Depression. Henry and Babette, untouched by the financial turmoil, hosted a little party at their Fifth Avenue apartment on the coldest day of the coldest January on record for New York City. It was more than the normal weekday lunch, more celebratory, more festive. There were Babette's favorite yellow roses and baby's breath in a silver basket at the center of the table and, at either end, silver étagères holding imported cherries and seedless grapes, sure to please Yehudi, the guest of honor, who was under the impression the party was in honor of his twelfth birthday. Aside from himself and his father, the other guests were the violinist Efrem Zimbalist, one of the reigning stars of the concert halls; Fritz Busch, the Philharmonic conductor; the Goldmans' daughter and sons and their wives and husbands; and Dr. and Mrs. Abraham Lincoln Garbat, who were old friends of both families. In lieu of joining them, Yehudi's mother had elected to take his two younger sisters skating in Central Park.

Garbat, who was Henry's personal physician, called on him every afternoon. He wasn't the typical Park Avenue doctor, more show than substance, in spite of the fact that he numbered Loebs and Lehmans and Lewisohns amongst his patients, as well as the

Goldmans. Dressed in a black derby hat and a black Melton over-coat even on the hottest summer day, Garbat had been a professional-caliber violinist by the time he graduated from Cornell University, but had been steered by pragmatic parents into the study of medicine. He and his wife, Rachel, lived in two adjoining houses on East Eighty-first Street between Park and Lexington Avenues,[1] using one as their home and the other as Dr. Garbat's offices, where he had developed a solid reputation as a diagnostician and a specialist in internal medicine and minor surgery.

They were patrons and friends of many of the most famous names in the New York music world in the 1920s, and their home was a friendly haven for visiting scholarship students from Palestine. They had become friendly with the Menuhins during their student days some ten years earlier and generously extended an invitation to the entire family—father, mother, Yehudi, and his two younger sisters—to stay at their home when they arrived in New York from San Francisco in order to further the boy's career and musical education. Garbat had known the boy since he was four and assured Henry he was "the real thing," not just another in the never-ending stream of fly-by-night prodigies.

Yehudi had made his first professional appearance in New York at the Manhattan Opera House at the age of nine.[2] He wore short black velvet pants and a white sweater that set off his rosy cheeks and blond hair, and was grinning from ear to ear. The recital was sparsely attended, but a number of well-known musicians were in the audience, including Walter Damrosch, the maestro of the New York Symphony Orchestra, as well as the fathers of young violin luminaries Mischa Elman and Jascha Heifetz, who undoubtedly attended in order to size up the competition. The artist was rewarded for his performance with a big bowl of strawberry ice cream.

Two weeks later he made his debut with the New York Symphony at Carnegie Hall. The auditorium was filled with a capacity crowd that had gathered as much out of curiosity as the conviction that no child could possibly interpret the extremely difficult program, which featured Handel's Sonata in E Minor and the first movement of Paganini's D Major Concerto, even if he were able to navigate all its technical demands. Members of the audience nudged one another when the boy first came on stage and passed his fiddle to the concertmaster for tuning because it was too great a stretch for his little hands. "But when the bow touched the strings, it was evident that an exceptional musical intelligence and sensibility, as well as uncommonly good technical groundwork, were behind the performance," wrote critic Olin Downes of the *New York Times*. "There was the silence that betokens the most intent listening until the cadenza of the first movement, when applause broke out and threatened to stop the performance."[3] When the concerto reached its finale, jaded members of the audience cheered and crowded to the stage, and the orchestra joined in the exuberant applause. Many in the audience wept openly as the boy played encores and waved acknowledgments to the orchestra and the critics went off to meet their deadlines.

When the billboards went up announcing Menuhin's first New York solo recital two weeks later, wild anticipation rippled through the city. It was the ticket of the moment, and everyone wanted in. Carnegie Hall was quickly sold out, packed from the orchestra to the last row of the galleries. Hundreds in the audience overflowed into the standing room stalls and onto the stage, where gilt-painted ball-room chairs provided extra seating. Many were classical musicians who had come to find out for themselves whether reports of the boy's extraordinary talent had been exaggerated. They were not disappointed.

Two years later, after Yehudi had furthered his studies with Louis Persinger in his hometown of San Francisco and made a few appearances in Europe, he was scheduled to perform once again at Carnegie Hall. The conductor of the orchestra, on loan from the Dresden State Opera, was the tall, elegant Fritz Busch, who was horrified to discover that "in this land of philistine entertainments it was not enough to be an outstanding conductor, one had to be Barnum as well."[4] Not only was he appalled to discover that maestro Walter Damrosch had arranged for him to play second fiddle to a child, he was aghast to learn that young Menuhin planned to include the Beethoven Violin Concerto, the most difficult piece in a violinist's repertoire, as part of his program.

"Can you imagine me being asked to back up a little boy?" he exclaimed to Henry when he came for tea the afternoon before the concert. The two men had met in Dresden some years before when Elena Gerhardt hosted the Goldmans for the opera season. "And even crazier, the child insisted on playing the Beethoven!" The idea was as ridiculous as having Jackie Coogan, the child movie star, play Hamlet, with Shirley Temple in the role of Ophelia! But both the boy and his father made such a fuss that Busch agreed to audition him at his apartment at the Gotham Hotel.

Busch could hardly contain his enthusiasm as he described his reaction to the boy's performance. "He played so gloriously and with such complete mastery that by the second tutti I was won over. . . . There were tears in my eyes. I threw my arms around him and told him he could play with me anytime, anywhere! Herr Goldman, you really must go tomorrow night, it will be a momentous occasion which you must not miss!"[5]

Although Henry held season tickets at Carnegie Hall, he had found some of Busch's programs a bit predictable that winter and had given this one a pass. But praise from Busch was praise indeed, and he instructed Schultzie to phone the box office and order the best seats in the house. If necessary, he would even pay scalper's prices. But there wasn't a seat to be had; not even standing room was available. He was so upset when he heard this that Busch gave him and Babette the use of his own personal box.

"The unparalleled success of Yehudi with the Beethoven concerto that night no one who was present will forget," Busch wrote in his memoirs.[6] One particularly tough critic remarked that this boy of eleven had proved conclusively his right to be ranked, irrespective of his years, with the most outstanding interpreters of Beethoven's music in the twentieth century. The review in the *New York Times* ran out of superlatives, saying, "Other children have accomplished technical feats, in the manner of trained dogs or intelligent seals, but [he has] a superb responsiveness to music . . . an uncommon intelligence, in a child."[7] Halfway through the program the audience threatened to hold up the performance with their applause and cheers. According to Menuhin's autobiography, *Unfinished Journey,* at the conclusion of the concert he tried to divert the audience's wild applause to Busch and to his teacher, whom he dragged on stage, but they would not let him go until he came out of the wings in his overcoat, his cap in his hand, rubbing his eyes and yawning.

For Henry, attending that concert was like the first chapter in a love story. The young boy's artistry inspired such depth of feeling in him, such soaring joy, that he was moved to tears. He had always wanted to be present when some cataclysmic event occurred, and now he felt his wish had been fulfilled. He was astonished to learn that the boy was playing on a borrowed instrument and decided without a moment's hesitation to give him a violin of his own. Dr. Garbat was asked to invite the Menuhin family to lunch at the Goldmans' after Yehudi's next New York appearance, but he was to keep the reason for the invitation a surprise.

Years later Menuhin could still recall arriving at the Goldmans' apartment overlooking Central Park and the Metropolitan Museum. It was "far more luxurious than any I had ever seen, its gold silk walls covered with Old Masters," he recalled. He found it "an education and an experience of unforgettable poignancy to be shown such riches by a man who saw their glories only with his mind's eye. He took us around his collection and pointed to the most minute and wonderful details of each painting, so well did he know them."[8] By then Henry had completely lost his sight.

Lunch was impressive, as well. Paul, the butler, had been instructed to uncork one of the few pre-Prohibition champagnes in the cellar, which was poured while deviled eggs and little nuggets of french fried eggplant were passed on a silver platter in the sun-filled living room. Yehudi was given a choice of grape or tomato juice. The meal was simple but beautifully presented: clear consommé, excellent roast chicken with tiny parsley potatoes and peas, and a marvelous dobos torte, the twelve-layered sponge cake filled and frosted with dark chocolate, which Mrs. Goldman said was the specialty of the house.

After the plates had been cleared away, Henry lit a cigar and addressed the guest of honor, who was seated next to him, in a casual, friendly tone. "My boy," he said, "I understand it is your twelfth birthday next week, a wonderful landmark in any young man's life. I should like to do something for you, something worthwhile that you will always remember. I would like to make you a present of a violin. You must choose any instrument you want, no matter what the price. Choose it—it's yours. What kind shall it be?"[9]

According to his autobiography, Yehudi already owned two very good violins and had been loaned a superb one by a wealthy patron in San Francisco, who had also paid for the three-quarter-size Grancino with which he had made his first New York appearance. But rave reviews aside, some critics had cast aspersions on the "rather poor instrument with limited capacities" on which he had played at his debut. Faced with such a fabulous offer, he wanted to settle for nothing less than the best. He didn't hesitate to respond, "A Stradivarius."

(It is interesting to note that just a few years later, Henry's eleven-year-old grandson Peter managed to catch himself on a metal hook while trying to lower the American flag at sunset in front of his grandparents' camp at Bull Point. It resulted in an ugly wound under his left armpit and required thirty-two stitches. Impressed by the boy's dry-eyed stoicism after the accident, Henry asked what he would most like to receive as a reward for his bravery. Peter quickly answered, "A case of Coca-Cola.")

From that moment on, there was no way Yehudi could contain his excitement. Over the next ten days, he and his father visited every violin dealer in the city, with the Goldmans' friend Zimbalist joining them in the hunt. By the end of the week, the youngster told everyone in sight that he had "just about made up his mind" which instrument he preferred. His father would not let him name it "for fear the price will shoot up," but he said that Yehudi had tested $300,000 worth of violins and that four of them were from the shop of the famous seventeenth-century craftsman of Cremona.

In a cramped rehearsal studio close to Carnegie Hall, Menuhin played each of the four violins in turn and then asked Zimbalist to try them out. Among those he turned down were several magnificent instruments, including the Betts Stradivarius, which was then being sold for $110,000 and is now in the Library of Congress.[10] The one with which he fell in love was called the Prinz Khevenhüller. It had been made for this nobleman in 1733 when Stradivari was ninety years old, and Yehudi described it as "ample and round, varnished a deep glowing red, its grand proportions matched by a sound at once powerful, mellow and sweet." But before making a final decision, he played Handel's "Prayer" on the Khevenhüller, then on the other three instruments, and one more time, on the Prinz again. "This is it!" he exclaimed joyfully. "I love it!" Zimbalist wiped the tears from his eyes and said, "Yehudi's right! It's the most marvelous

Strad in the world. But then, Yehudi is the most marvelous violinist of our age. They deserve each other!"[11]

According to the *New York Times,* the price tag was $60,000, which included the valuable Tourte bow that Menuhin used throughout the rest of his career. However, the dealer's receipt read, "To Yehudi Menuhin—in trust of his father Moshe Menuhin . . . one violin . . . known as the 'Prinz Khevenhuller' . . . $48,000." Word on the street had it that Moshe pocketed the difference, assuming that Henry, being blind, would not notice. Whether or not this was true, Henry never questioned the sum and said it was a privilege to be the donor, knowing the pleasure the world would receive from listening to Yehudi play.

Henry and Babette, always extremely averse to publicity, had hoped to remain anonymous. But it was difficult to keep such a magnanimous gift under wraps, so it was decided to make a very low-key announcement at the Garbats' home as part of their young daughter's birthday celebration. After the presents had been opened and the ice cream and cake devoured, Fifi borrowed her father's top hat and cane, seated the guests in a semicircle, and performed a funny little skit she had written in French. Her friend Yehudi, apparently unaware that the gift of the Strad was making headlines, lay splayed out on the floor, chuckling and joining heartily in the applause. It made his father happy to see him out of the spotlight for a change, and not the focus of everyone's attention. Of course, that would never have been the case if his mother, surprisingly absent, had been there. In her eyes, there was only one star in the firmament . . . and one "Mama" to run the show.

In stark contrast, a few blocks south on Wall Street, the party that was the Roaring Twenties was over. After the end of World War I, business at Goldman Sachs had continued to languish and new IPOs failed to materialize. With no family member expert in the field of underwriting, it was clear that someone would have to be hired from outside the firm to fill Henry's shoes. In a master stroke of misguided inspiration, the partners settled on a handsome, smooth-talking southerner, a classmate of Paul Sachs at Harvard Law School who was in the munitions purchasing department at J. P. Morgan. As it turned out, Waddill Catchings appeared to have been more of an Elmer Gantry, a master huckster, rather than a gifted financier.

In the next few years, as Wall Street flourished and the economy prospered under the leadership of Calvin Coolidge, Catchings organized such great companies as National Dairy Products, an amalgam of several large regional firms, and the Postum Cereal Company, in which he gathered Jell-O, Maxwell House Coffee, and a variety of other famous brands, and renamed it General Foods.[12] But as one triumph followed another, he became domineering and imperious, demanding a larger percentage of the firm's ballooning earnings and elevation to the role of senior partner. It was a position that had never before been assumed by anyone outside the family, and Arthur Sachs, the partner who had championed bringing him aboard in the first place, began to question whether the man should be given free rein and control of the other partners.

Riding the crest of his success, insistent on being the ultimate authority, Catchings, who had come from very modest beginnings, now looked at his bankbook and found himself very, very rich—at least on paper.[13] But not as rich as he wanted to be. It was then that he originated the concept of the Goldman Sachs Trust, the Shenandoah Corporation, and the Blue Ridge Corporation, a group of closed-end mutual funds. They sold like hot cakes. From day to day their prices leaped by tens and twenties; doubled and split and doubled again. Greed feeds on greed, and the man in the street couldn't get enough of the trusts; it seemed that there was no limit to their upside. In an age of speculation, they were the darlings of the market.

Now Walter Sachs, who had heard his Uncle Henry say that "money is always in fashion" more than once, began to suspect a lack of transparency in Catchings's high-flying investment vehicles. However, when he expressed concern about what appeared to him to be nothing more than a pyramid scheme, Catchings brushed him off. "The trouble with you, Walter, is that you've got no imagination," he sneered. "This is the biggest deal Goldman Sachs has ever had!"[14] Walter ruefully observed in hindsight, "Most men can stand adversity; very few men can stand success."

Catchings's house of cards collapsed, and the investment house crashed in October 1929, setting the stage for a worldwide depression. All its paper profits disappeared, along with those of its clients, and $121 million of its value—half of which represented the partners' own investment—vanished within a year. Many of the firms' shareholders were completely wiped out, and the lawsuits brought by clients charging fraud and neglect were so numerous that Wall

Street wags used to telephone the Exchange Place office and ask for the "litigation department." The firm became the butt of jokes in music halls and cabarets, to the embarrassment and dismay of the principals, who had sworn to maintain its pristine reputation, come what may. Among the infuriated shareholders was comedian Eddie Cantor, who had invested heavily when times were rosy. A favorite Depression-era shtick of his was a sketch satirizing the Jewish prayer for the dead in which the "corpse" was the Goldman Sachs Trading Corporation.

Henry's personal resources remained untouched by the debacle. He had steered clear of any participation in the trusts, considering them far too risky. Since leaving the firm, he had committed most of his capital to conservative railroad bonds, the booming CIT Financial Corporation (which had become the prime lender in the ever-expanding automobile industry), and the thriving May Department Stores assemblage of retailers. But when he heard through the grapevine that Catchings had come up with still another wildly suspect scheme by which he planned to cover Goldman's losses and raise millions on questionable convertible notes, Henry could not help but feel chagrined, observing the depths to which "the great old firm to which [he had] given his all" had fallen. Aloof and secure at his homes on Fifth Avenue and in the Adirondacks, he voiced no compassion for the dire situation facing his relatives and erstwhile partners. When he heard that his nephew Walter had said the firm could have stopped the hemorrhaging of capital if they had just been a little smarter, or a little less greedy, he couldn't have agreed more.[15]

Meanwhile, Babette and Henry's lives had begun to revolve increasingly around the career of Yehudi Menuhin. Like aging camp followers, no distance dissuaded them from attending his performances, much to the vexation of the boy's mother, who regarded them as interlopers in her family's private life. They lavished attention on him as if he were a favorite grandchild rather than the beneficiary of their philanthropy. They were among the first to purchase tickets for his initial concert in Berlin, in 1929, which attracted such mobs to the ticket line that the management of the concert hall summoned the police to head off potential rioting.

The international press reported that at the end of the performance Albert Einstein leaped onto the stage from his seat in the audience, embraced the young artist and cried out, "Now I know there is a God in heaven!"[16]

When Yehudi spent the next summer in Switzerland, studying with conductor Fritz Busch's brother, Henry and Babette rented a chateau nearby and arranged frequent picnics and little excursions with him in their chauffeured touring car. More often than not, his teacher was included in the party, but they were always told his parents and his sisters were "unavailable" or "otherwise engaged." By the end of six weeks, Yehudi was calling the old gentleman "Uncle Henry," although Babette was formally addressed as "Mrs. Goldman" and Busch remained "Herr Professor."

Babette, not insensitive to the rebuffs, decided in the spring of 1930 to try smoothing the waters with Yehudi's possessive mother by inviting the entire Menuhin family, Yehudi's parents and little sisters Hepzibah and Yaltah as well as the boy himself, to be their

Henry and Babette in Baden-Baden, their favorite summer retreat

guests for two weeks at Baden-Baden, the Goldmans' favorite watering spot, before he began his second summer tutorial. The Bavarian resort was a showcase of everything Henry loved most in Germany[17]—clean sparkling air and the smell of pine woods; orderly flower beds neatly arranged down every walkway; starched white bedsheets changed every day by smiling, rosy-cheeked mädchens, rich Austrian food and baccarat tables for gambling in the evening. But when the Menuhins arrived at Badrutt's, the poshest hotel of the posh, one can only assume that Yehudi's mother found it far too elegant and reserved for the family, and she chose to have them stay instead at a small pension in the village. Badrutt's was a

"Uncle Henry" and Yehudi on a morning stroll in Baden-Baden

resort for the elderly and wealthy and had little in common with life in the real world, she told the children.

It would be the last opportunity for Henry to enjoy a time of quiet intimacy with his protégé, for the young man would soon turn sixteen and embark on a series of lengthy worldwide tours. While they were in Baden-Baden, Yehudi made a habit of calling for Uncle Henry early in the morning, and they took long walks together, stopping along the way for hot chocolate and *Schnecken* at one of the coffeehouses. Hepzibah and Yaltah, who themselves were blossoming as piano prodigies, would sometimes join them on an afternoon to listen to a band concert in the park, and from time to time Babette would treat them all to ice cream or a tea party after she emerged from her treatments at the spa.

By 1936, Florence and Robert and Junie were becoming concerned by what they perceived as an excessive amount of attention being showered by their parents on Yehudi. Money was not the issue, except perhaps for Robert, who had emptied his pocketbook considerably chasing after women. Ed Vogel, Florence's husband, had made a sizable fortune of his own, advancing to the vice presidency of CIT, and Junie enjoyed a flourishing career as a Wall Street specialist, making a market in retail issues and ensuring that their trading was orderly and protected from wild fluctuations. What bothered them was the seeming lack of interest by their parents in their own children's development, and they eagerly looked forward to renewing family ties during the month of August at Bull Point.

It was almost as if everyone knew that the summer of 1936 would be the final one, and the camp was swamped with guests for lunch. Dr. Holt from a neighboring camp brought Helen Keller and her teacher, Annie Sullivan, to visit Grandpa, who had inherited a soft spot for aiding the deaf from his father. A real queen, Marie of Romania, whom Granny had met at the spa at Marienbad, spent a weekend and brought gypsy costumes for the girls, and for me, an autographed copy of a children's book she had written. The Texas department store magnate Stanley Marcus paid a call and fascinated us with the collected plays of Shakespeare, which he had had printed privately in tiny leather-bound volumes. The college boy waiters from Wawbeek next door paddled over and challenged the young men at our camp to a canoe tilting contest, which we won, and Professor Einstein brought his wife, who was ailing and picked at her food.

And then there were the musical guests. They gossiped a lot about their colleagues, where they were touring, what they were performing, whether their range was up to their roles. And, of course, who was sleeping with whom. They professed not to spend much time with others in the musical world, saying they found it "so refreshing" to mingle with people like the Goldmans who could talk about something besides music. And yet that was all that really interested them.

The Wallensteins, of course, were different. Virginia and "Wally" were best friends of my parents, and one would never guess that he was a world-class cellist, mentored by the famously temperamental Arturo Toscanini, and soon to become a symphony conductor himself. Affable and outgoing, he was often mistaken for a stockbroker or a surgeon and loved discussing literature, economics, and world affairs with my grandfather. Virginia was an exceptionally pretty blonde, a pianist, and handled her role as Wally's public relations representative with ineffable skill and charm. They reciprocated my grandparents' generosity by inviting my mother, Adrienne, to join them on the Los Angeles Philharmonic's goodwill tour of Japan when she was widowed twenty years later.

CHAPTER TEN

End of the Line

*"Ultimately we have to set our own criteria for what constitutes fail-
ure and what constitutes success. It's not the same for everyone."*

—Henry Goldman's advice to his sons

When they returned from the mountains in the early autumn of 1936, Henry retained a cautious view of the nation's economy. The state of international finance, which depended so heavily on the United States, was bleak indeed, and the world was still reeling from the domino effects of the Great Depression, which had been triggered by the stock market crash of 1929.

The Federal Reserve's gold supply, on which the dollar was based, had dwindled alarmingly despite the new president's legislation to ban private ownership of gold, and nine thousand banks had failed in the United States alone, unable to collect loans from their debtors. One brokerage house after another had declared bankruptcy as investors reneged on paying the calls on their margin accounts, which encouraged them to purchase securities for just 10 percent of their value. Capital investment and construction had come to a virtual halt, and prices and incomes had fallen by 20 to 50 percent.

It was clear that a fresh viewpoint was needed, and Roosevelt appeared to be the man who could provide it. The state of the Union was beginning to show improvement. Henry was supportive of the New Deal programs designed to alleviate the highest unemployment rate in history, such as the Works Progress Administration and Civilian Conservation Corps, and to provide relief to the unemployed with passage of the Social Security Act. However, he disagreed thoroughly with FDR's policies of government intervention in private industry and the president's heavy-handed stands against big business.

At the same time, Hitler and Mussolini officially joined forces, Germany and Japan signed a military pact, and a few months later, Hitler's forces marched into the Rhineland, which the Versailles Treaty had declared a demilitarized buffer zone between Germany and France, and spread westward to aid Franco's fascist brigades in toppling the Spanish Republican government. In sports, Jesse Owens won an unprecedented four gold medals at the Berlin Olympics in 1936 and Joltin' Joe DiMaggio became the newest pride of the Yankees. In December, King Edward VII of England abdicated his throne to be with the woman he loved, and the beloved "little tramp" Charlie Chaplin let his voice be heard in a film for the first time. And for Henry, it was nearly the end of the line.

Anyone could see that he was not his usual engaged, energetic self. His breathing became increasingly short and his sleep was fitful. Dr. Garbat, a daily visitor, said he was suffering from myocardial infarction, a progressive form of heart failure. His ankles began to swell and he felt too enervated to go for his customary walks on Fifth Avenue. But in spite of his waxy pallor, with Schultzie's help he tried to keep up appearances. Neatly shaved and barbered, he sat for hours in his leather easy chair, lovingly fingering the Cellini inkwell that graced his desk, waiting for the arrival of his afternoon callers. His secretary, John Schwartz, brought the office mail after lunch, Brodnitz read him the daily papers and museum publications, and Granny would while away the time, feeding him tidbits of gossip while she worked at her needlepoint. He loved to listen to her caricatures of the Wall Street wives who were her friends, many of whom had affected speech idiosyncrasies that they considered "teddibly smaht" and high society.

As Henry viewed his imminent mortality, frustrated by his waning ability to participate in wrestling with the problems of the world, his thoughts could not help reverting to the Goldman Sachs he had known and helped build to greatness years before. It was starting to make a comeback, but it would be a long haul. The Great Depression had swept away much of its capital reserves, and the firm had lost in excess of $10 million in the Catchings trusts alone. But he held no sympathy for them. They had relied on the decisions of others, which he himself would never have done. His only concern was the restoration of Goldman Sachs's good name and reputation and the public's faith in its integrity.

As for making peace with his sisters and the Sachs family, even since Sam's loss of memory as he grew old and his subsequent death several years earlier—this was not a part of his agenda. They had been out of his life for almost twenty years.

His views of the current economy, though it seemed to be improving somewhat since the inauguration of Franklin D. Roosevelt, was pessimistic. Although the president's administration was creating temporary jobs with work programs like the WPA and the CCC, and at the same time improving roads and parks and irrigation projects across the nation, Henry felt they quashed big business, which could have spawned new enterprises and created better-paying, permanent employment over the long term.

Henry also feared for the future of Germany, even as America pursued a collision course that would lead inevitably to another world war. The two nations could have made such a great team, he thought, with Germany providing the brains and the United States the brawn. But Hitler's swift rise, and the totalitarian state that the German people had embraced with astonishing relish, made the realization of his wishes utterly impossible.

Henry shared with Babette, his closest confidante, the regret that he had never developed greater rapport with his children, who respected and admired him, but who turned to her and her sister Rose to share confidences and seek emotional support. It seemed to run in his family, he thought, this inability to "noodle" with them, to express approval of their baby steps toward maturity, to overlook their minor slips, to embrace them and say, "I love you." Conversely, he could become intimate with virtual strangers within moments and talk about any subject they chose—art, finance, philosophy, politics, music—just so long as it didn't touch on anything personal. A similar reserve did not seem to cling to the Loebs and the Schiffs and the Lewisohns and their large, seemingly happy families.

As the rose-colored Sèvres clock on the mantel struck five, he would invariably turn to faithful Schultzie and ask, "When's Joe coming? . . . It's getting late. Where's Joe?" Duveen, by this time suffering from an advanced stage of cancer, which he refused to acknowledge to either clients or friends, always went out of his way to stop in before dinner with news of the Rialto, but his legendary tardiness had not abated with time.

There were other friends who came to see him, too, among them Fritz Kreisler, Alma Gluck, the flamboyant publisher Alfred Knopf and his wife, Blanche, who was writing a cookbook, *Cook, My Darling Daughter.* Chocolate confections arrived in the mail from Europe and sweet-smelling flowers from the Madison Avenue florists. Rosie, Henry's sister-in-law, prepared her famous pickled herring for him every Friday (he hated the sole and flounder that Babette ordered for "fish day" out of respect for the servants' Catholic dietary strictures, complaining that they were full of bones), and his daughter Florence brought him the latest recordings of Wagner's love duets. Junie frequently made a detour on his way home to share the latest rumors and rumblings on Wall Street, and one day Henry's ten-year-old granddaughter June composed a waltz, "The Bull Point Waltz," on the big black Steinway in the living room and dedicated it to him. And yet there was a void deep inside him begging to be filled. His dying wish was to hear Yehudi Menuhin play the Beethoven Violin Concerto one more time.

The Menuhin family was living in Paris at the time, and Yehudi was enjoying a well-earned rest after a year of nonstop touring. In a few months' time the family would return to the States, unable to stomach living with the sense of privilege accorded an international star while friends and fellow musicians in Berlin, Dresden, Vienna, were being denied a livelihood and had been deprived of their civil liberties and worldly goods. The Germans had even banned the playing of the great composer Mendelssohn's work because he was Jewish, prompting Yehudi to turn down an invitation by conductor

Wilhelm Furtwängler to play with the Berlin Philharmonic and "restore the breach between Germany and the world of music and art."[1]

But after the Christmas holidays "Aba," chafing at the dwindling family finances resulting from his son's little sabbatical, contracted for Yehudi to record several Bach concertos with his former teacher, the Romanian fiddler George Enescu, in New York, and to make a guest appearance with the National Broadcasting Company's symphony orchestra. Virginia Wallenstein, whose nose for news in the music world was unsurpassed, couldn't wait to tell Babette, who immediately sat down at her desk and wrote Yehudi a note. It had never been the Goldmans' style to ask for favors or to expect reciprocation for their generosity, and so it never entered her mind that the young violinist might turn her down when she invited him to call and told him how much his playing would brighten Henry's last days.

When Yehudi showed the letter to his mother and told her how pleased he would be to make "Uncle Henry" happy, Marutha, always jealous of his relationship with the Goldmans, flew into a rage. It was out of the question, she shouted; the idea didn't even warrant discussion! From the very beginning she had vowed that she would never permit her son to play anywhere but in a concert hall, especially not for patrons or royalty, and there was nothing that would make her change her mind. Yehudi could do as he wished once he was out on his own and married, but for now she, and she alone, would decide where he would play, and where he wouldn't.[2]

It is difficult to believe that a twenty-year-old superstar who was applauded and revered around the world would be afraid to antagonize his mother. But apparently the iconic artist with the touch of an angel had feet of clay. When Yehudi walked up Fifth Avenue to say his goodbyes, his Stradivarius stayed at home.

Henry's death came on tiptoe, without much fanfare, in much the same low-key style he had maintained throughout his incredible life. He and his beloved Babette were marveling about their ability to read each other's minds, like old members of a symphony orchestra who had rehearsed together for years. Suddenly his head dropped to his chest and the conversation stopped. Babette rang for Schultzie. The butler, Paul, telephoned Dr. Garbat and asked him to come at once. A fabled life had ended for the Renaissance gentleman whose ethics and morals never ran second to ambition and drive.

In the newspapers it was reported that Henry Goldman, the legendary progenitor of investment banking, died on April 4, 1937, in his Fifth Avenue apartment, surrounded by the paintings and sculptures he loved.[3] They described him as "one of the outstanding figures of the modern industrial and financial world" who had developed "a modern method of industrial financing for commerce and industry." In a day when there were no personal computers, no Internet, no e-mail or even adding machines, when business was developed solely with talent, imagination, and brains, he was responsible for the initial organization of many of America's most successful publicly owned corporations, including the General Cigar Company; Sears, Roebuck & Co.; the Underwood Typewriter Company; May Department Stores; the Studebaker Corporation; Stern Brothers Department Store; F. W. Woolworth; Cluett Peabody; B. F.

Goodrich; Jewel Tea; and the Brown Shoe Company. Until his retirement from Goldman Sachs in 1917, he was a hands-on director of all these concerns, for which he did not accept any pay.

In the days immediately after his death, the public learned more about Henry Goldman than they had ever been permitted to know while he was alive. They read in the papers about his philanthropies, his groundbreaking innovations in the world of finance, the evaluation of his paintings, and the bequests in his will, and heard radio newscasters conjecturing on the key to his successes. But the man himself remained an enigma to the thousands of people whose lives he had influenced and changed.

Investment banking, in part his legacy to the world of finance, survived intact for over a hundred years and only came to be truly challenged as a result of the economic meltdown of the early twenty-first century. One cannot help but wonder how he would have felt about the transformation of Goldman Sachs into a publicly owned entity and, subsequently, a bank holding company regulated by the Federal Reserve, in which there are a hundred partners and a billionaire investor from Nebraska is the owner of a hefty portion of its preferred stock. I don't think he would have agreed with Salomon Brothers' former chairman who, in taking that respected old partnership public in 1981, remarked that "the main effect of turning a partnership into a corporation [is] to transfer financial risk to its shareholders. When things go wrong it's their problem."[4]

A perennial champion of the gold standard, Henry viewed it as a bulwark against runaway government spending, and for years he cautioned governments, corporations, and his own family about the perils of relying on "soft money." He held little sympathy for those who lost everything because they insisted on living beyond their means. There would have been no seat in his boardrooms for venture capitalists and hedge fund managers of the here and now whose primary goal has been to grow their bank accounts by making money from money, regardless of the impact on society. He never forgot where the buck stopped, and where responsibility lay.

Among the many letters of sympathy received by the family was one from Sidney Weinberg, who had been elevated to the position of partner in Goldman Sachs in 1927 and assumed the role of senior partner five years later. Weinberg had started his career with the firm as a porter's assistant, an eighth-grade dropout whose chores included cleaning the office spittoons, brushing off the partners' boots, and filling the office inkwells. For a long time he was known around the office simply as "boy." But like Henry, whom he greatly admired and viewed as one of the geniuses behind the success of Goldman Sachs, Sidney was an excellent listener and an adaptive student. In 1919, upon his separation from the Coast Guard, in which he had served as a cook on board Junie's boat *Babette II* during World War I, he approached Henry seeking a job. Henry advised him to return to Goldman Sachs. That was where opportunity lay, and Henry was not planning to go back into the investment business. Demonstrating once again a canny talent for spotting human potential, he offered to act as Weinberg's mentor and to introduce him to valuable contacts in the business and social worlds. One of his first steps was to invite the young man to serve as a groomsman at the wedding of his son Junie, much to the bride's rather snobbish dismay.

At Goldman, Weinberg became a salesman of commercial paper for $28 a week plus 1.8 percent in commissions. Henry advised him to ask for a bigger piece of the pie as his sales escalated, and he advanced to earning 33 percent at a time when the stock market was booming. Under Henry's guidance, he formed syndicates to sell underwritings, to determine the pricing of new issues, and to supervise trading. And in the thirties, Henry recommended and endorsed him for seats on many of the corporate boards on which he would serve for almost forty years. After the departure of Waddill Catchings, Weinberg joined Walter Sachs as co-chairman of the firm, became a trusted advisor to presidents and corporate chairmen, and was generally credited with steering Goldman Sachs into a revitalized era of prosperity and stature.

Not surprisingly, there was no word of condolence from any of the Sachses, not even Henry's sister Rosa (whose husband, Julius Sachs, had passed away three years earlier), or his nephew Walter, who directed the daily activities of his staff from one of the two senior partners' offices at Goldman Sachs. The Goldman family of my generation, in fact, had never met any of them, and was unaware of how our family trees were intertwined. They were not a subject of discussion at our dinner table nor were there likenesses of them in any of the photo albums my mother and grandmother thumbed through whenever the last bits and pieces of our clan gathered for an occasion. My only recollection of seeing Grandpa's sister Louisa was once, many years later, when she had a chance meeting with my grandmother in the elevator of New York's swank Hotel Pierre, where both of them lived. She was a tiny little sparrow of a woman with snow white hair, dressed in black from head to toe in mourning for her daughter Ella, who had died in childbirth in the distant past. Granny, by contrast, looked like a page out of *Vogue,* wearing a sable jacket over something gray and diaphanous, a John Fredericks hat, and her celebrated pearls. They exchanged cool nods and went their separate ways. A stranger might have assumed they had met once or twice at a fund-raising event or a tea, and would never have guessed that, in fact, they were sisters-in-law.

Some of the contemporary Sachses professed they didn't even know they "were Goldmans." The rumor is that the legacy of discord would manifest itself among the Sachses for years and would live on in the stories of family members along with tall tales of everything from the wages Henry paid his servants to a sighting of him marching in a pro-German parade during World War I.

From an early age, Henry had been taught that it was a privileged part of the German Jewish heritage to care for others who had been blessed with less than themselves. Following in the philanthropic footsteps of his father, who had been a major donor to Dr. James McCune Smith's "colored children's asylum" and a school for deaf mutes on Manhattan's West Side, Henry devoted a great deal of time and money during his lifetime to universities, hospitals, libraries, and organizations such as the American Association for the Blind, the University in Exile, the Central Committee of German Jews, and the Jewish Federation. His only proviso was that they never use his name. He wanted to see his donations at work while he was still alive, he said, and specified in his will that after he died additional funds from his estate would not be made available to them. Many of the causes he elected to support, such as the establishment of physical education facilities in New York public schools and the creation of an experimental agricultural station in what was then called Palestine, were generally overlooked by the circles in which he moved.

It wasn't until that last unhappy visit to Berlin, when he was confronted with raw anti-Semitism, that he came to terms with his feelings about Judaism. He had always believed, like his friend Professor Einstein, that the Jews were a coalition of tribes united by their ethnicity and a common belief in one omnipotent God in whose image we are all created, but he had disassociated himself from formalized religion of any sort long, long ago. Nevertheless, he clung to the belief that German-Jewish bankers in America, who had the money to finance welfare schemes and the political clout to bring them to fruition, needed to step up at that moment in history and assume a role of leadership in assuring European liberals and Jews safe harbor and sustenance. In his final days, he called in all his chips, writing hundreds of letters to his influential contacts at home and abroad, providing appeals and affidavits for scientists, scholars, physicians, artists, and authors attempting to flee from the impending Holocaust.

Perhaps most heroically, Henry and Babette lent a helping hand to refugee children, some of whom arrived, frightened and alone, and found their first American home at his camp on Saranac Lake. I still have fond memories of playing with Brigitta and Ulli, a German sister and brother around my own age who stayed with us at Bull Point one summer. I sometimes wonder still what became of their lives in the United States after their escape from Germany.

A simple ecumenical memorial service was held at 10:30 in the morning at the Goldmans' apartment a few days later. Fritz Kreisler played some of Henry's favorite compositions on the violin, and Florence sang the *Ave Maria* that Henry had always loved. As the rabbi from Temple Emanuel intoned, "The Lord is my shepherd; I shall not want," Babette, dry-eyed and composed, prayed that her husband would see in all its shining details the new world laid out to challenge and delight him when he completed his journey through the valley of death. It was difficult to imagine that this warm, intelligent woman would, within a few years, be afflicted with the same hardening of the arteries as her sister Rose.

Robert, arriving barely on time, bobbing and smiling with his characteristic charisma, was insistent on demonstrating his most recently acquired camera to the assembled mourners and took candid shots of his mother from every conceivable angle before the service began. In his eulogy he spoke of the stony silence that had greeted him when he was caught misbehaving as a boy and how his father had always reminded him that you are judged by the company you keep. A little chuckle escaped him as he looked back on his marital escapades and wondered if Henry had used them as a reference point.

Junie, the son who had tried hardest to emulate Henry, recalled Henry's remarkable ability to size people up within moments, to determine whether they were the real thing or "full of baloney." He spoke admiringly of the Old World courtesy with which his father had always conducted himself, socially and professionally. If a man could be summed up in just a few words, Junie said, the speech from

Hamlet would best describe his father: "This above all, to thine own self be true. And it must follow, as the night the day, thou canst not then be false to any man." The mourners were not a sentimental lot. The ladies powdered their noses and fanned themselves with their hats and the gentlemen glanced at their watches. Junie was the only one to shed a tear.

The rabbi closed by asking the small assembly of intimate friends and family to join him in reading the Lord's Prayer. Henry had asked Babette to make the service short and sweet, and she had planned the arrangements exactly according to his wishes. The whole thing was over in less than half an hour.

The cortege braved the noontime traffic and slowly drove over the Fifty-ninth Street Bridge to Salem Fields, the Jewish cemetery that lies on the border of Brooklyn and Queens. A tall stone wall separates it from the Catholic Mount Carmel cemetery to the east, and a Protestant cemetery lies to the west. The whole area, covering well over a square mile, is a testimonial to the dead, united in their segregation.

The Sachs mausoleum crowns one of the highest hills in Salem Fields. Flowering dogwoods, magnolias, and fruit trees flank the entrance. Here lie the ashes of Samuel, his daughter, his brother Harry, and his sister-in-law Edith. Eventually they were to be joined by Louisa, his brother Barney, and other members of the family.

Fifty yards down the hill, closer to the cemetery entrance and the fast-paced city traffic, is the final resting place Henry had built for himself and his heirs. It is larger and grander, and its back is turned on the Sachses in death as in life. Like a sentinel, a huge tree stands by the steps leading to the entry, guarding the privacy that Henry preserved so zealously throughout his life. He was a man who had never been convinced that he had achieved all his goals, or that he had reached the summit in his journey through life. He would undoubtedly find it rather amusing that, in modern times, the firm he influenced so greatly is referred to simply as "Goldman," although no Goldman has worked there since 1917. And it is unlikely one ever will again.

Afterword

*T*hose who remember my grandfather say he was a moralist who often said it was a pleasure to make money, and even more of a pleasure to see that money used to make the world a better place. He was eager to help new industries thrive and grow, and in so doing give the public access to innovative products and opportunities that would modernize and enrich their lives. From the early days of his youth he was fascinated by the future, and no new discovery in science or industry failed to engage his interest.

I cannot help but wonder to what further heights the family firm might have soared if he had remained a managing partner in the decades before it went public, despite his complexities. Would it have linked up with Lehman Brothers once again and become a leading underwriter for the emerging industries of the twenties, thirties, and forties—airlines, motion pictures, television, computers, rocket science? Had things been otherwise, perhaps Goldman Sachs would never have become a publicly traded company and instead remained a closely held partnership.

Thinking about all this, I went back to Bull Point not long ago. It was a crisp autumn day and I hoped to bridge the gap between yesterday and tomorrow. The leaves reflected in the navy blue water were just starting to turn crimson and gold. The last time I had said goodbye, Granny was standing on the dock waving her scarf and yodeling "Tra La La Hoohoo!" to the last departing guests as

George steered the *Babette* away from the shore. Since then, there had been a number of raging forest fires in the region, one of which completely destroyed the camp except for the boathouse, and, of course, the memories.

Now, as our little outboard approached the camp, gunshots rang over the bow and she was splattered with spray, spurring our curiosity as to what secrets might be hidden there. Clearly, visitors were not welcome. We were later told that the property, which Henry's estate had bequeathed to Mount Sinai Hospital, had sub-

The boat house, the only remains of Bull Point Camp

sequently been purchased by a Colonel Edwards and his wife, who operated it as a boys' summer camp, and that it was rumored to have been turned over once again for development as a motel complex. We also heard from a hiking guide that elk had returned to the area and that UFOs had been sighted dipping over what once had been Bull Point Camp.

Looking at images in the old photo albums, it is hard to believe that all of these people are gone now, along with their smiles and songs, will and wisdom, and fears and hopes for the future.

$\mathcal{N}otes$

CHAPTER 1: AGAINST ALL ODDS

1. **"Men can learn from the past":** The reminiscences of Walter E. Sachs, 1954, in the Oral History Collection of Columbia University (hereafter OHCU).

CHAPTER 2: BANKING IN "THE SWAMP"

1. **Marcus hung out a shingle:** Stephen Birmingham, *Our Crowd* (New York: Harper & Row, 1967), p. 87.
2. **a tiny office in a basement:** Ibid.
3. **carried his commissions in the band of his hat:** Ibid., p. 88.
4. **the city's number one boys' college preparatory school:** The school, no longer in existence, was folded into the Franklin School around 1912, and Julius Sachs became a professor of secondary education at Teachers College at Columbia University several years earlier. Reminiscences of Walter Sachs, OCHU.
5. **The firm's name was changed:** Lisa Endlich, *Goldman Sachs: The Culture of Success* (New York: Knopf, 1999), p. 33.
6. **"one of the most brilliant social events of [the] season's social history":** *New York Times*, January 21, 1890.

CHAPTER 3: THE GOLDMANS AND THE SACHSES

1. **when his firm's annual sales of commercial paper had doubled:** http://www.associatedcontent.com/article/1560711/the_dow_jones_industrial_average_barometer.html.
2. **"the famous Sachs temper":** Anonymous family source.
3. **"Goldman Sachs is one firm":** Stephen Birmingham, *Our Crowd* (New York: Harper & Row, 1967), p. 24.
4. **recycled money was dirty and full of germs:** Family source.
5. **died, reportedly of syphilis, at the age of forty-five:** Private family letters.
6. **Jacob Schiff was fascinated:** Birmingham, *Our Crowd*, p. 160.
7. **"did not wish to tarnish the firm's good name":** Lisa Endlich, *Goldman Sachs* (New York: Knopf, 2005), p. 38.

8. Goldman Sachs would come up with the clients, Lehman the money: Ibid.
9. It was Henry's belief that retail stocks could be calculated by their earning power: Ibid., p. 28.
10. it is the most widely used method for assessing the value of a security: Ibid., p. 39.
11. Annual sales climbed: Sears Archives.

CHAPTER 4: GOING PUBLIC

1. She vehemently declared that she had been "framed up": *New York Times,* January 7, 1915.
2. As guardian for his underage son: Ibid.
3. Edith, smiling sweetly: *New York Times,* March 3, 1915.
4. "going around visiting New York banks": Reminiscences of Walter Sachs, OHCU, April 4.
5. first man he called on was J. Ogden Armour: OHCU, p. 25.
6. "cock of the walk": Ibid., p. 26.
7. "I've never forgotten that [you were] so nice": Ibid., p. 27.
8. "Money is always in fashion": Ibid., p. 27.

CHAPTER 5: WAR IN THE BOARDROOM

1. Julius Forstmann of the woolen merchant family: The reminiscences of Walter Sachs, 1954, in the Oral History Collection of Columbia University (hereafter OHCU), p. 37.
2. "a turning down office": Lisa Endlich, *Goldman Sachs* (New York: Knopf, 2005), p. 41.
3. all the likely suspects were sitting right there: Ibid.
4. "link up to a new engine to forge on": Elena Gerhardt, *Recital* (London: Methuen, 1953), pp. 77–78.
5. "to which I have given all that is in me": Endlich, *Goldman Sachs*, p. 43.
6. "an extraordinary personality, the original genius": Walter Sachs, OHCU, p. 56.
7. "a man well regarded": Walter Sachs, OHCU.
8. Medical observers were summoned: http://www.firstworldwar.com/source/abdication.htm.
9. the private train of Supreme Allied Commander Ferdinand Foch: www.gutenberg.org/etext/17511.

CHAPTER 6: PHOENIX RISING

1. But all was silence from the Trianon Palace: Margaret MacMillan, *Paris 1919* (New York: Random House, 2002).
2. If the Allied powers failed: Ibid., p. 464.

3. "You asked us for peace": Ibid.
4. "a treaty which is falling down over their own heads": *New York Times,* August 5, 1922.
5. overprinted almost hourly with more zeroes: John Weitz, *Hitler's Banker: Hjalmar Horace Greeley Schacht* (Boston: Little Brown, 1997).
6. could not accept the terms of the Versailles Treaty: Ibid.
7. "[our] only remedy is to attract foreign capital into German industry": Ibid.
8. he found fault with the Dawes Plan: *New York Times,* August 4, 1924.
9. "I was especially impressed by the President's keen interest": *New York Times,* April 21, 1922.
10. "The future of the German financial system is far from rosy": *New York Times,* December 16, 1924.
11. "they believe in it. I don't": Kai Bird and Martin J. Sherwin, *American Prometheus* (New York: Knopf, 2005), p 64.
12. "Einstein is completely cuckoo": Ibid.
13. "Permit me on behalf of Mrs. Goldman and myself to thank you": Letter, Goldman to Einstein, February 7, 1924, courtesy of the Goldman family.
14. "I [gave] a series of three lectures": Reminiscences of Walter Born, OHCU.
15. Hedi (Mrs. Born) received forty large packing cases, sent from America: Max Born, OHCU.
16. He was unquestionably the most popular leader in the history of the German people: William Shirer, *Berlin Diary* (New York: Knopf, 1940).
17. On his fiftieth birthday, in March 1929, it seemed as if the whole world wanted to help him celebrate: Walter Isaacson, *Einstein: His Life and Universe* (New York: Simon & Schuster, 2007).
18. He was emphatic in telling them that he would never return: Ibid.
19. His every move was recorded: Ibid.
20. supported patriotic militarism as vigorously as Einstein spoke out: Ibid.
21. "during war . . . [science] gave people the means to poison and mutilate": Ibid.
22. "Because of Hitler, I don't dare step on German soil": Ibid.
23. "Your safety in America depends on your silence": *Einstein for the 21st Century,* ed. by Peter L. Galison, Gerald Holton and Silvan S. Schweber (Princeton, NJ: Princeton University Press, 2008).
24. Einstein was walking a slender tightrope: Ibid.
25. In a subsequent letter to Henry: Courtesy of the Albert Einstein Archives, Hebrew University of Jerusalem, Israel.
26. "If I were to attempt to give you a picture": Letter, Henry Goldman to Julius Goldman, April 13, 1933, courtesy of the Goldman family.
27. A gang of Hitler Youth students and beer-hall thugs: Shirer, *Berlin Diary.* Courtesy of the Albert Einstein Archives, Hebrew University of Jerusalem, Israel.

28. **"A fifteenth century reign of terror exists there"**: Letter, Henry Goldman, courtesy of the Goldman family.

29. **"Who cares if half a million Jews are killed?"**: It was, in fact, Ian Johnson, refugee commissioner of the League of Nations and head of the Foreign Policy Association, who was told by Hitler in an April 8, 1933, interview, "I will do the thing that the rest of the world would like to do. It doesn't know how to get rid of the Jews. I will show them." Ian Johnson, *Advocate for the Doomed* (Bloomington: Indiana University Press, 2007).

30. **"Dr. Luther never made this remark to me"**: Henry Goldman to Einstein, January 3, 1934, courtesy of the Goldman family.

31. **hosted a burning of books by Jewish authors**: *Jewish News Weekly,* September 29, 2006.

CHAPTER 7: THE FINE ART OF COLLECTING FINE ART

1. **Neither man tried to pretend**: S. N. Behrman. *Duveen* (New York: Little Bookroom, 2002).

2. **"It was moving to see him amongst his pictures"**: Oral History of Max Born, American Philosophical Society.

3. **"If you're going to spend a quarter of a million"**: Behrman, *Duveen*.

4. **At length he became threatening**: Duveen Archives.

5. **"I am now its happy owner"**: Letter from Goldman to Berenson, February 13, 1924.

6. **"tell Mr. Goldman to let anyone he likes write about his Fra Angelico"**: Behrman, *Duveen*.

7. **"I was intensely mortified"**: Letter from Goldman to Duveen, 1916.

8. **"one of the finest bronzes"**: Letter from Duveen to Goldman, 1921.

9. **he joked with Henry about his not needing any advice**: Letter from Duveen to Goldman, 1921.

10. **"I have been in Paris two weeks"**: Letter from Goldman to Duveen, 1921.

11. **Henry and Babette had been in several times to see "the Titian"**: Duveen Bros. Paris to Duveen.

12. **"Your remarks about the enhancement of the value"**: Letter from Goldman to Duveen, 1925.

13. **"raining Titians"; "It looks as though"**: Letter from Goldman to Duveen, 1925.

14. **"I can, of course"**: Letter from Goldman to Duveen.

15. **"The new fellows are usually young"**: Letter from Goldman to Duveen, 1928.

16. **"My dear Joe, let me give you"**: Letter from Goldman to Deveen.

17. **"This is exactly what I expected"**: Letter from Duveen to Goldman, 1928.

18. **"Be cautious"**: Letter from Goldman to Duveen, 1929.

19. **"Here in America"**: Letter from Goldman to Duveen, August 1936.

20. **"Is he broke?"**: Meryle Secrest, *Duveen* (New York: Knopf, 2004).

CHAPTER 8: BULL POINT CAMP

1. It was built in the sophisticated style of an English Tudor country house: Harvey H. Kaiser, *Great Camps of the Adirondacks* (Boston: Godine, 1982).

CHAPTER 9: A CHILD PRODIGY

1. two adjoining houses on East Eighty-first Street: Yehudi Menuhin, *Unfinished Journey* (New York: Fromm, 1997).
2. his first professional appearance: Lionel Menuhin Rolfe, *The Menuhins: A Family Odyssey* (San Francisco: Panjandrum, 1978).
3. "There was the silence": *New York Times,* November 26, 1927.
4. "in this land of philistine entertainments": Fritz Busch, *Pages From a Musician's Life* (London: Hogarth Press, 1953).
5. "He played so gloriously": Ibid.
6. "The unparalleled success of Yehudi": Ibid.
7. "Other children have accomplished technical feats": *New York Times,* January 1927.
8. "far more luxurious than any I had ever seen": Yehudi Menuhin, *Unfinished Journey* (London: Macdonald and Jane's, 1978).
9. "My boy . . . I understand it is your twelfth birthday": Ibid.
10. Among those he turned down: Ibid.
11. "Yehudi's right!": Ibid.
12. Catchings organized such great companies: Reminiscences of Walter Sachs, OHCU, 1954.
13. Catchings, who had come from very modest beginnings: Ibid.
14. "The trouble with you, Walter": Ibid.
15. the firm could have stopped the hemorrhaging: Ibid.
16. "Now I know there is a God in heaven!": Rolfe, *Menuhins.*
17. a showcase of everything Henry loved: Menuhin, *Unfinished Journey.*

CHAPTER 10: END OF THE LINE

1. "restore the breach between Germany and the world of music and art": Lionel Menuhin Rolfe, *The Menuhins: A Family Odyssey* (San Francisco: Panjandrum, 1978).
2. she alone, would decide where he would play: Ibid.
3. died on April 4, 1937: Obituary, *New York Times,* April 5, 1937.
4. "the main effect of turning a partnership into a corporation": *Wall Street Journal,* "Bankers Need More Skin in the Game," February 25, 2009.

Index